TALES FROM THE

TORONTO BLUE JAYS

DUGOUT

A COLLECTION OF THE GREATEST BLUE JAYS STORIES EVER TOLD

JIM PRIME

SPORTS
PUBLISHING

Sports Publishing books may be purchased in bulk at special discounts for sales promotion, corporate gifts, fund-raising, or educational purposes. Special editions can also be created to specifications. For details, contact the Special Sales Department, Sports Publishing, 307 West 36th Street, 11th Floor, New York, NY 10018 or sportspubbooks@skyhorsepublishing.com.

Sports Publishing® is a registered trademark of Skyhorse Publishing, Inc.®, a Delaware corporation.

Visit our website at www.sportspubbooks.com.

10 9 8 7 6 5 4 3 2 1

Library of Congress Cataloging-in-Publication Data is available on file.

ISBN: 978-1-61321-640-8

Printed in the United States of America

To Jeff and Jung and Catherine and Dave.
And to Sam and Fin. And to Glenna.

CONTENTS

INTRODUCTION

It was a full week after April Fool's Day, 1977, but Mother Nature still clung stubbornly to the spirit of that day, as if this was some gigantic prank being played on baseball and Canada.

Dressed in a red parka, Canada's songbird Anne Murray sang *Oh Canada*—although her signature tune *Snowbird* might have been more appropriate for the occasion. Fittingly perhaps, the Toronto Blue Jays, Canada's American League representatives in the summer game, were hatched in -2 degree Celsius weather. Ironically, later that evening the Toronto Maple Leafs, iconic symbols of our winter game, would be playing the Pittsburgh Penguins indoors in the cozy comfort of Maple Leaf Gardens.

Dave McKay, the only Canuck in the Jays' original lineup, admitted later that he had "goose bumps" when Murray sang our anthem, ignoring the fact that it might just as easily have been a touch of frostbite. In fact, Goose Bumps might have been a better name than Blue Jays for Toronto's fledgling American League franchise. The name Blue Jays had actually come via a Name the Team contest in June and July of 1976. There were more than 30,000 entries and more than 4,000 different suggestions. The winning name was suggested by 154 people, and there was a drawing to decide the winner. On August 13, 1976, the new franchise was officially dubbed the Toronto Blue Jays.

The blanket of snow threatened to postpone the April 7th game that fans had waited an eternity to see. In the pregame hijinks, Jack Brohamer of the visiting Chicago White Sox used a pair of catcher's leg pads as cross-country skis. Two Louisville Slugger bats served as his ski poles. But the sell-out crowd of 44,649 didn't seem to mind that the diamond was more white than green. They were Canadians, after all, and this was Mother Nature's way of letting everyone know that the game can be just a little different north of the 49th parallel. Anything else would have been positively un-Canadian. And speaking of un-Canadian, the stands at Exhibition Stadium were devoid of beer due to a ridiculous ruling by the province of Ontario. The first franchise cheer wasn't "Let's go, Blue Jays," but "We want beer!" Despite the lack of suds, fans were intoxicated with the spirit of the occasion, happy that Toronto had finally fielded a Major League Baseball team. The last time a professional team had played in Toronto was ten years earlier when the Toronto Maple Leafs of the International League last took the field to represent the city. The Leafs subsequently moved their operations to Louisville, Kentucky.

At precisely 1:50 p.m., the frosty air ensured that umpire's cry of "Play ball!" could be seen in puffs of exhaled air as well as heard. It announced that Canada now had an American League franchise to balance out the National League's Montreal Expos. Doug Ault was the hero of the day, hitting the first two home runs in Jays' history and thereby writing the first line in his future obituary, in Canadian newspapers at least. But on this day he was very much alive, and the *Toronto Star* headlined THE BIRTH OF THE BLUE JAYS with an accompanying picture of Ault's home run swing. "The fans really got me pumped up," the 27-year-old Texan told reporters after the game. Despite his southern roots, Ault had played for the Anchorage, Alaska Glacier Pilots so was no stranger to cold weather. The first homer was a solo shot over the 375 sign in left field. The next was hit over the right field fence just inside the foul pole. The Jays pounded out 15 hits and won the game 9-5. Everything they did was a first. The first win went to reliever Jerry Johnson. The first pinch hit homer was struck by Alvis Woods in his first Major league at-bat. The first Canadian to get a hit for the Jays, as well as the first Canadian to get two hits, was McKay.

Ticket prices at Exhibition Stadium ranged from $6.50 (Canadian dollars) for Field Level Chairs to $5.00 for Upper Level Chairs to Right Field Reserved Bench at $3.00 to First Base reserved Bench at $4.00. General Admission cost you a two-dollar bill. This was pre-toonie, after all. The Jays sold 8200 season tickets for anywhere from $500.50 to $231.00

Manager Roy Hartsfield tried to lower expectations by stating the obvious. "[This team] won't set the world on fire," he said. That original team of green rookies—the average age was 26—was supplemented with a scattering of cast-offs and over-the-hillers. The entire team payroll was a modest $800,000.

They are forgettable except for the fact that they are totally unforgettable. They are the original Blue Jays, who finished the season 45 games behind the NY Yankees with a record of 54-107. It would only get worse for the new franchise. In 1979 they managed only 53 victories against 109 losses and finished 50 ½ games out of first. That season's lowlight was a 24-2 drubbing laid on them by the California Angels.

Much has happened since that singular moment in Canadian sports history. Sadly, the Expos have moved on to Washington and are now the Nationals. Canada's baseball pride is now the exclusive preserve of the Toronto Blue Jays. The Jays won their first division title on October 5, 1985, in a game against the vaunted Yankees. The names on that roster are infinitely more meritorious than those on that historic 1977 log, names like George Bell, Ernie Whitt, Willie Upshaw, and Lloyd Moseby. Bell made the final putout on a fly ball, dropping to his knees in a display of unbridled emotion after the catch. More titles and more near misses followed. Early season snow—what DH Cliff Johnson called moose dandruff—continued to fall on the Jays until finally, in 1989, the Jays left their nest at Exhibition Stadium and settled into a spectacular aviary, known as SkyDome. In their new climate-controlled environment, they went on to win back-to-back World Series championships in 1992 and 1993. The first had the entire country spellbound. Ontario premier Bob Rae even claimed to have made a wager with Governor Zell Miller, his counterpart in Georgia.

"I made him a bet . . . I offered if we lost we'll give him the CN Tower and if he loses, they'll give us the [1996] Olympics."

Following the pair of World Series victories there were declines and disappointments, rebuilds and reloads, all tempered with great team and individual accomplishments.

Some of the players in this book will be well known to you; others may have been long forgotten or escaped your notice entirely. Together they tell the story for the Blue Jays in a very personal way, from A to Z—specifically from Danny Ainge to Gregg Zaun.

What's in a name? The Blue Jays have had a Baker (Dave), 2 Butlers (Rick and Bob), 3 Carpenters (Chris, David, and Drew), 3 Coopers (Brian, David, and Don), 4 Millers (Dyar, Justin, and Trever), a Painter (Lance), a Milner (Brian), and a Shepherd (Ron). They have had a Fielder (Cecil) and a Glover (Gary), a Walker (Pete) and a Homer (Homer Bush). They had Jimmy Rogers and another Singer (Bill) and to accompany them, a Viola (Frank) and 2 Bells (George and Derek). They had a Lennon (Patrick) but sadly no McCartney. They have had 2 Greens (Nick and Shawn)—4 if you add an 'e' at the end—, a Brown, and a White. They have had a Mench, a Sharperson, a Wise (DeWayne), a Klutts (Mickey), and a real McCoy (Mike). They have had a guy who was a Leach (Rick), another who was Lawless (Tom), and a third who was Gross (Gabe). They boasted two Musselmans (Musselmen? Jeff and Ron). Some players became household names: they had a Roof (Phil), one Storey (Mickey), a Lamp (Dennis), a Stairs (Matt), a Key (Jimmy), 4 Wells (David, Greg, Randy, and Vernon), 2 Bushes (Dave and Homer), a Pond (Simon), and a Creek (Doug). They have had a definite Edge (Butch) and once in the Service (Scott), were always ready to Battle (Howard), possibly with a Cannon (Joe). For

American history buffs they had a Quantrill (Paul) and a Rader. They also had 2 Lewises (Fred and Rommie) and 2 Clarks (Bryan and Howie). They have had 9 Johnsons (Cliff, Dane, Jerry, Joe, Josh, Kelly, Reed, Tim, and Tony) and one Wang (Chien-Ming) but strangely only 3 Smiths. As they evolved they had a Darwin (Danny) and for those with a classical bent, they acquired Virgil (Ozzie). Botanists enjoyed watching Crabtree (Tim). They had a Swann (Pedro). They have had an entire League (Brandon). They even had George Costanza's nemesis, Steve Braun. They have had a Thigpen (Curtis). And a Kawasaki to make sure the good times continue to roll.

Not all of these colorful players appear in the following pages, but I hope that those who do will reflect the relatively short but glorious history of Canada's Team, the Toronto Blue Jays.

DANNY AINGE

Perhaps if the NBA Raptors were around in the early eighties, he'd have been part of that Toronto sports franchise. Sadly, they were not, and Toronto fans were forced to watch him play baseball instead. His career batting average was .220, and he hit a total of two major league home runs in parts of three undistinguished seasons with the Toronto Blue Jays. Nevertheless, Danny Ainge is one of the more recognizable names in the early history of the Toronto franchise. The Eugene, Oregon, native was a first team high school All-America athlete in football, basketball, and baseball and went on to star in basketball and baseball at Brigham Young University. For his hard court achievements, he was named the NCAA's National Player of the Year and winner of the prestigious John Wooden Award.

The Blue Jays selected him in the 1977 amateur draft, and he played his first games for the Jays in 1979 while still in university. In fact, he remains the youngest player ever to suit up for the Jays (20 years and 77 days when he debuted). He split his playing time between second and third base with a few forays into the outfield.

* * * *

After three pretty miserable seasons (he batted .187 in 1981), Ainge decided that his future lay in hoops, not hits. In an interview with *Sports Illustrated* writer Jack McCallum, he admitted, "I've failed at things before. I think I've failed at baseball the last three years. I've set goals for myself, and I haven't come close to them. If I keep failing for a certain period of time, I'll definitely try something else. Basketball? Probably." But before he could hit the basketball court, he had to hit the

US District Court in a legal battle between the NBA's Boston Celtics, who had selected him in the 1981 draft, and the Jays. Eventually the Celtics prevailed and Ainge became a footnote in Jays history.

* * * *

The court case provided an unlikely cross-sport battle that spawned great animosity between the two pro franchises. Testimony was given, indicating that Ainge had verbally informed the Blue Jays brass of his desire to leave the team and that he had received a verbal okay from Peter Bavasi. "You have to do what you have to do," Bavasi allegedly had said to Ainge, adding "No contract could make a man do what he doesn't want to do." The contract had explicitly banned Ainge from playing pro basketball, in exchange for a $300,000 bonus. Ainge offered to return the bonus. The Blue Jays discounted the verbal exchange as being off-the-cuff remarks uttered in haste and with no legal bearing. Bavasi compared the situation to "an ailing wife being left behind by her husband for some blonde floozy from Boston."

* * * *

The initial court proceeding was a victory for the Jays, and after it was over—in a symbolic gesture that any Boston basketball fan would instantly recognize—Bavasi lit up a large cigar. This was the trademark courtside tradition of Celtics legendary coach, general manager, and president Red Auerbach when a victory was considered to be in the bag.

Bavasi boasted, "There's one minute to go and we're 20 points ahead. As far as I'm concerned, Danny Ainge is a member of the Toronto Blue Jays." Countered Celtic vice-president Jan Volk, "The thing is, they don't even want him, and he doesn't want to be there. We shouldn't have to buy their franchise to get him."

The legal dispute was eventually settled, and Ainge began a successful 14-year playing career as a Boston Celtic. He is currently President of Basketball Operations for the Celtics.

* * * *

Paul Hodgson was a former roommate of Ainge's in Toronto. "Danny and I talked a lot about his situation. It was baseball vs basketball. On the very first day of spring training, *Sports Illustrated* showed up with a photographer and General Manager Pat Gillick was given a fungo bat. Danny went to third base, and Gillick threw the ball up in the air and hit it toward third base. The cameras were flashing and the ball took a bad hop and hit Danny in the mouth for about 12 stitches. I mean there was blood everywhere. It was crazy. It was as if he'd cut his aorta. That was the end of the shoot for the day and the end of the interview for the day. The ball wasn't hit particularly hard. It just hit the right rock in the right spot. *SI* didn't use the pictures. Today it would have gone viral. That was Danny's first day in spring training.

"Danny was being rushed to the majors, that's for sure. I never thought he had the conviction that baseball would be the game for him. He gave it his best because he was a competitor and good all-around athlete, but it was not where his heart was."

* * * *

Hodgson recalls the interaction between the rookie Ainge and veteran John Mayberry. "Mayberry was ruthless to him on the bus. He ribbed him about being a skinny white kid trying to play in the NBA. Mayberry's old neighborhood in Detroit was filled with NBA stars, and he'd gleefully list them for Danny. John would just go on and on about it. 'No way you could have hung in my neighborhood,' he'd say. It was supposed to come down to Mayberry and Ainge shooting hoops for money, but it never happened because if it had, I would have been the first one there to watch it.

"That's another example of Big John making a guy who was in a tough, pressure-packed situation feel welcome and allow him to laugh at himself. Ainge was getting a lot of big league press then and he wasn't a big leaguer—certainly not an established big league baseball player by any stretch. John made him laugh and it was appreciated by Danny, he told me so."

DOYLE ALEXANDER

Featuring more arm angles than a Boy Scout semaphore class, Doyle Alexander was a finesse pitcher all the way. Released by the New York Yankees after a sub-par 1982 season and a poor start in 1983, Alexander came to the Jays via free agency in June of that year. He had nowhere to go but up, and that's exactly the direction he headed, albeit gradually. He posted a 7-8 record on the strength of a 3.93 ERA.

The Jays really got their money's worth the following year, as Alexander went 17-6 with a 3.13 ERA. He completed 11 of the 36 games he started.

In 1985, fans could hardly wait to see which Alexander would show up, and while it may not have been Alexander the Great, it was certainly Alexander the Pretty Darn Good. Posting another 17-win season (against 10 losses), he maintained a 3.45 ERA. Even though he struck out a meager 142 batters in 260 innings of work, he kept opposition hitters off balance with his baffling array of deliveries and speeds. With a stellar defense behind him, it was a happy marriage. Alexander's reliable mound work helped lead the Jays to their first postseason appearance. Once there, the bubble burst, as the Jays were beaten by the

Kansas City Royals in the ALCS. Alexander's ERA ballooned to 8.71 in his two starts.

* * * *

Doyle Alexander was the winning pitcher for the Blue Jays when they captured the first division title in the Jays' short history on October 5, 1985. Fittingly, the clincher came against the New York Yankees at Exhibition Stadium. Ironically and satisfyingly, Alexander's previous team—those same Yankees—were still paying most of Alexander's $800,000 salary.

ROBERTO ALOMAR

"Growing up in the San Francisco area, I was able to watch Willie Mays and I was also able to cover Roberto Alomar during his days here in Toronto," announcer Jerry Howarth details. "They are the two best ballplayers I've ever seen. I say

AP Photo/Elise Amendola

that because of the way they play in all areas of the game. They had a sixth sense for the game that some very few are just blessed with. Those two had it. They knew how to win and could beat you with anything from a bunt, to a home run, to a defensive gem.

"Roberto is one of the nicest human beings I've ever met. It all went part and parcel with winning and he covered a position and a half out there at second base and it was a delight to watch.

"Everyone remembers the John Hirschbeck incident. In my opinion, that's what makes a Hall of Famer on and off the field. How do you come back from adversity? He had made his mark on the field and it was an ugly incident, a black stain on Roberto's career at that point.

"After Robbie was dealt to Cleveland, a wonderful thing happened. John Hirschbeck lived in the Cleveland area and his kids love the Cleveland Indians and as a result when Roberto became a member of the Cleveland ball club, the kids said to their dad, 'What do we do?' and he said, 'Let's get together.' The result was that one of the umpire's attendants there brought Roberto together with John in a game that he umpired against Cleveland. John brought his family and Roberto was so extremely disappointed with himself and sincerely apologized to John.

"John had lost a son to a rare disease and Roberto said, 'Not only do I want to be your friend for what I did, but I want to help you raise money for a cure, to help other kids who are in the same situation.' They became friends and they are friends to this day and they respect one another. That's how you come back from adversity. That's how you respect people in the game—not for what they do well but for how they come back from things they don't do well. It's real life. That's why I have the greatest respect for Roberto Alomar."

* * * *

Few infielders have ever defended their little patch of ground with the vigor and skill that Roberto Alomar brought to the post. That's why the motto of his countless fans might well be "Remember the Alomar!" In 1994, the *Scouting Report* said of the Toronto second baseman: "Roberto Alomar really doesn't need to get any better—but he keeps doing it anyway." Now that the dust has finally settled around his keystone position, Roberto Alomar can lay legitimate claim to the title "best second baseman of his day" and arguably "the best of all time."

* * * *

Of the countless vivid images that are summoned when Roberto Alomar's name is mentioned, many are centered on second base, where he was a magician. His conjuring, rabbit-from-the-hat defense amazed and stunned fans. He turned certain hits into outs and turned double plays with presto-change-o ease.

But lest you think his magic was limited to defense, he had unlimited offensive cards up his sleeve too. Was it the greatest home run in Blue Jays history? No, Joe Carter has that one all wrapped up and tucked away. But it certainly makes the short list. It was Game Four of the 1992 ALCS against the Oakland Athletics. The game was in the ninth inning and the Blue Jays were losing 6-4 with colorful, cocky, dashing, swashbuckling Zorro-like Dennis Eckersley on the mound for the A's. Eckersley had won the Cy Young Award and American League MVP award the previous season, so despite the fact that he had coughed up two eighth-inning runs on singles to John Olerud and Candy Maldonado, A's manager and acknowledged baseball genius Tony LaRussa made no move to the bullpen. His faith was rewarded, as the man they called Eck registered the third out, a strikeout of Ed Sprague. As he left the mound, he turned toward the Blue Jays dugout and defiantly pumped his fist.

The gesture did not go unnoticed by the Jays. In fact, it was like waving a red flag in the face of a bull. "It woke us up," Derek Bell said later. "We jumped off the bench and yelled back at him." If it had been audible to the TV audience, viewers of the exchange would have heard more bleeps than back-to-back episodes of *Trailer Park Boys*. After the game, a smiling Joe Carter surmised, "Maybe he forgot he had to pitch the ninth." To which Robbie Alomar added, "He thought he had stopped the bleeding."

After all, during the regular season, Eckersley had accumulated more saves than a pre-intervention participant on *Hoarders*. Of the 54 save opportunities he was presented with, he succeeded in 51 of them. In short, LaRussa could scarcely be faulted for having a high level of confidence in his relief ace. So what if he had blown a save the previous night? All the more incentive for this fiery competitor. Who better to face the top of the Jays' potent lineup than the brash, Errol Flynn-channeling right-hander? Not only that, but the A's had been an astonishing 82-1 during the season in games where they held the lead after eight innings.

But Errol Flynn was about to go from dashing to dashed. Devon White singled and scrambled to third when the ball skidded past left fielder, and future Jay, Rickey Henderson. Alomar stepped into the batter's box. Later he told reporters, "I remembered Kirk Gibson did it to him. Why not me?" (He was referring to Gibson's inspiring pinch hit homer off Eckersley to win Game One of the 1988 World Series for the underdog LA Dodgers against these same A's. Gibson had injuries to both legs and literally hobbled to the plate to deliver the winning blow.) The second baseman worked the count to 2-2 and then sent the next pitch, a fat fastball over the heart of the plate, high and deep to right. As it fell into the stunned crowd, he soared around the bases, his unrestrained joy all the more striking because of the funereal pall that he had single-handedly cast over the patrons of

Alameda County Coliseum in Oakland. Eckersley walked a few steps off the mound and stood watching, in apparent shock. The score was now 6-6 and Eck was a wreck.

Extra innings followed, and the Jays eventually won it in the 11th frame on a Derek Bell walk followed by a single by Candy Maldonado that put runners on first and third with none out. After Kelly Gruber lined out to first, Pat Borders hung a rope to left field and Bell tagged up and easily beat the throw. The Jays held the A's scoreless in the bottom of the frame. But the home run against baseball's best fireman is what everyone remembers about the game. "Ol' Eck stuck it to us and gave us a good reason to come back and stick it to him," said gloating Toronto starter Jack Morris. "The poor guy wouldn't look over at us when he didn't strike Alomar out. Little League stuff." The win was crucial for the Jays and helped to catapult them past the A's in six games. Alomar confessed in his book *Second to None,* "That was the best game I ever played in my life in baseball." Anyone who saw it would have to agree.

* * * *

One of the few low points of Alomar's Hall of Fame career came in the form of some not so great expectorations. The incident is one of the few black marks against the seemingly squeaky-clean player that every woman in Toronto either wanted to marry or mother.

Now a member of the Baltimore Orioles, Alomar was facing his former team on September 27, 1996. He argued a called third strike with umpire John Hirschbeck and lost his temper. The end result was that Alomar spat in the umpire's face. He then compounded the offense by telling reporters that Hirschbeck was "bitter" because his son had recently died of ALD. Hirschbeck was understandably incensed at this insensitive remark and Alomar was suspended for the first five games of the following season. He was very remorseful and donated $50,000 to ALD research. The two combatants ultimately shook hands and have become friends.

"We have done some things with charity," said Alomar when he retired. "God put us maybe in this situation for something."

* * * *

Roberto Alomar could steal home and then steal home, all without going outside. Alomar's home for much of his time with the Blue Jays was a room at the SkyDome Hotel.

* * * *

ALEX ANTHOPOULOS

If he is, indeed, a magician as many people have suggested, he's more from the Pat Gillick school of magic than the one attended by Harry Potter, which of course is Hogwarts. When Alex Anthopoulos took over as Senior Vice President of Baseball Operations and General Manager of the Blue Jays in 2009, the Jays were an empty hat and few people knew what the new leader might be able to pull from it. He waved his wand and Presto, there appeared Brett Lawrie. Chango—there is Brandon Morrow. Then Colby Rasmus. Following a brief intermission, he hit his stride in the off-season prior to the 2013 campaign, adding Jose Reyes, Melky Cabrera, R. A. Dickey, Mark Buehrle, and so on.

Too early to say if the moves were truly magical or just smoke and mirrors.

J. P. ARENCIBIA

Tom Hanks, eat your heart out. J. P. Arencibia possesses a flair for the dramatic that rivals anything the two-time Academy Award winner could muster. And his timing is perfect. His debut performance was positively Forrest Gumpian in terms of its unlikely script. He arrived in the major leagues on early August 4 and played his first game on August 7, 2010. It's not a day he's likely to forget. Nor will Blue Jays fans. Playing against the Tampa Bay Rays, he had the kind of entrance that you dream about when you're a card-collecting, gum-chomping, wide-eyed, hero-worshipping kid. First time up, first pitch he had ever seen in the big leagues, he clubs a Jamie Shields delivery over the out-field barrier for a two-run homer. Only 27 players in the long history of baseball had ever homered on the first offering they had seen. Where do you go from there? Well, allow me tell you.

Next time up, he doubled, followed in order by a single and—yes, another homer. At this point he had to be thinking, *This Major League Baseball stuff is a piece of cake.* His 2-homer performance put him on a list of only five players to ever go deep twice in their major league debut. "It's nuts," he told the *Lion's Den University.* "I don't really think about it, then when I see highlights, I get chills. It's still hard to believe."

* * * *

The following 2011 season was his official rookie campaign. Once again, J. P. made both a grand entrance and a grand encore. As the starting catcher in the Jays' home opener, he homered twice and stroked a triple.

* * * *

On Opening Day of the 2012 season, once again Arencibia became the hero, this time with a three-run homer in the 16th inning (record for the length of an Opening Day game in MLB history) to defeat the Cleveland Indians.

* * * *

Arencibia rates Justin Verlander as the toughest pitcher he has faced. Nevertheless, he was the one who destroyed Verlander's hopes of a perfect game on May 7, 2011, outlasting the pitcher in a grueling 12-pitch battle to draw a walk.

* * * *

Arencibia has a talent for channeling NHL hockey players' postgame interview banter. After a recent game, he talked about going "top shelf" after hitting a home run. When asked about what he'd want to be if he wasn't playing baseball, his response was immediate: "NHL enforcer."

* * * *

Asked by *Lion's Den U* which pitcher, in the long history of baseball, he would most like to catch, he replied, "Babe Ruth, and take him out for a few beers."

* * * *

The media hype about the newly minted 2013 Blue Jays was waaay over the top. Arencibia put things into perspective after the Opening Day loss to Boston at the Dome. "Unfortunately, my dream of 162-0 is not going to be real," he said.

* * * *

While Arencibia came in with a bang, he left with a whimper. The likeable catcher had a terrible 2013 season, batting .194 with an on-base percentage of .227. When Dioner Navarro was signed, J. P. was no longer in the Blue Jays' plans and moved on to the Texas Rangers.

ALAN ASHBY

In a major league career that extended from 1973 to 1989, Alan Ashby caught for the Cleveland Indians, Toronto Blue Jays, and Houston Astros. He was the other half of the battery during no-hitters by Ken Forsch, Nolan Ryan, and Mike Scott. Ashby went on to become the partner of Jerry Howarth on the Blue Jays broadcast.

He still has fond memories of his time as a Blue Jay. "In 1977, Rick Cerone was the starting catcher," he told SABR's Maxwell Kates. "All spring long there were rumors that I was going to be traded to the Angels for Ron Jackson. The Blue Jays kind of went about that entire spring that I wasn't going to be a part of the team. So we got into the first week of the year. Cerone was still the catcher and I was still supposed to be traded. About a week or nine days into the season, they decided the trade wasn't going to happen. Cerone got sent to the minors and that's how I got to play."

* * * *

Among his most vivid memories of playing in Toronto was the first game the new team ever played on Canadian soil—or snow. He recalls the terrible weather and the final decision to go ahead with the game. "I knew we were playing. I had heard that at any cost we were playing that day. [Broadcaster] Tony Kubek was around with the national TV [station] at the time. He said, 'Oh, get ready boys, you're going to be playing.' It really didn't matter if it was snowing, they were going to get it going at some point. I still wasn't sure how long I was going to be in that uniform. It was probably warmer in Anaheim."

* * * *

Despite the cold and snow, Ashby appreciated the warm welcome extended by fans to the fledgling team. He also recalls the first Blue Jays manager and his inspirational clubhouse sessions.

"Roy Hartsfield was one of those managers who had a lot of clubhouse meetings. I'm not a big fan of clubhouse meetings, but Roy was funny. He would start out very mellow and very Georgian in his approach and tell us a bunch of old Georgia-isms to start with. Before long, almost 100 percent of the time, the veins in his neck [stuck out]... and it would finish with 'And if you're not proud to play with this uniform ...' The uniform at home said 'Blue Jays' and the one on the road said 'Toronto' and invariably, he would get it wrong every time. 'If you're not proud to wear this uniform that says (blank), we'll get somebody else to do it.' You knew that was the closing to the meeting."

DOUG AULT

First baseman Doug Ault was not a star ballplayer. He was, at best, a journeyman and may have never made it to the big leagues if it had not been for expansion. Nevertheless, he will forever hold a special place in the hearts of Blue Jays fans. When the Blue Jays played their very first game on April 7, 1977, Ault became an instant hero for the baseball-starved populace of Ontario. The label was attached in the bottom of the first inning when the 27-year-old rookie first baseman attacked an 0-1 pitch and sent the ball over the wall of Exhibition Stadium, to the rapturous delight of the capacity crowd of 44,000 fans. As an encore, he homered in his second official at-bat as well and hit four in the first four games of the Jays' existence. Three years later, he was gone from the Blue Jays and out of the majors for good.

* * * *

Ault once worked on an oil rig in the North Sea. He had had some experience on Louisiana oil fields, and, short of funds during a vacation in England, thought he'd give it a try.

* * * *

Ault was a rarity, a left-handed thrower who batted from the right side. Usually it's the other way around. He was a switch-hitter when he was in his mid-teens and said, "I always seemed to hit better right-handed, so I stuck with that." Ault was a southpaw pitcher in junior college and once started and won both ends of a doubleheader, the first one 1-0 in 10 innings and the nightcap 2-1 in 11 innings.

* * * *

The Doug Ault saga has a tragic ending. Just three days before Christmas of 2004, the deeply depressed former ballplayer died of a self-inflicted gunshot wound in the driveway of his Tarpon Springs, Florida, home.

BOB BAILOR

Bob Bailor was the Jays' first legitimate shot at a player of the year, the guy they hoped to build a team around in 1977. He was the first Blue Jays pick—second overall—in the expansion draft and became their first player of the year, leading the team in hits with 154 and stolen bases with 15. His .310 batting mark set a new standard for an MLB expansion team player. He was also named to the Topps all-rookie team despite not having a defined defensive assignment, 53 games at shortstop being his longest stint at one position. He captured player-of-the-year honors in 1978 as well.

* * * *

The most impressive thing about Bailor was his versatility. He was a jack of all trades and master of many. He covered third base, shortstop, and all three outfield positions and even took a few turns on the mound. The first such appearance came in 1980 in a desperation move when the Jays didn't want to further deplete the bullpen in a lopsided game. In total he entered three games in an emergency relief role.

* * * *

On April 20, 1977, Bailor struck out for the first time as a major leaguer. He had survived 52 at-bats until the Yankees' Sparky Lyle finally rang him up. The following year he struck out just 21 times in 621 at-bats as the everyday right-fielder. In 1979 his average slipped to an anemic .229, with a lone home run and 38 RBIs. His defense was more impressive. He had 15 outfield assists to tie him with Boston's Dewey Evans for the AL lead that year.

* * * *

Bailor did not like to lose, but with an expansion franchise, it was inevitable. He once admitted to the *Globe and Mail* that it sometimes wasn't easy to maintain his optimism. He once told Alan Abel, "I'm standing out there in the outfield and it's the second inning and we're down three or four runs already, and I just think, 'Aw geez, here we go again.' Then you find yourself behind, 14-0, and you stand there and say, 'God, hurry up and get this over with.'"

* * * *

Bailor became known as the "Leetle Mon," as opposed to veteran Rico Carty, who was "The Beeg Mon." The nickname was born when Bailor was being interviewed on CBC and Carty walked up and placed his chin on the shorter man's head. "This is the 'Beeg Mon' speaking to you from behind the 'Leetle Mon,'" he said. The name stuck.

JESSE BARFIELD

W ho can forget the golden arm of Jesse Barfield unleashing laser-beam throws from the deepest recesses of right fields throughout the American League? Barfield combined with Lloyd Moseby in center field and George Bell in left to form what has often been called the best defensive outfield of the 1980s.

As radio broadcaster Jerry Howarth said, "Bell, Moseby, and Barfield—what a trio. They were the building blocks for the Blue Jays future. They were young, they were talented, they were enthusiastic. They all brought different skills and talents to the table to help the Blue Jays win, but they also played together so well. They were always positive, they were upbeat, they were learning as they went. They wanted to get better and they brought everyone along with them. And they also borrowed from the veterans to make themselves better as well."

In truth, it was Moseby and Barfield who earned the defensive plaudits. They also earned one of the most colorful dual nicknames in the game, bestowed by teammate John Mayberry: Shake and Bake.

* * * *

It was Jesse Barfield who bridged the rookie-veteran divide that once existed on the Blue Jays. "Jesse was the changing of the guard," recalls Paul Hodgson. "In 1980, Barfield was in camp as a roster player, and he started playing his boom box. Rookies didn't play music, it was an unwritten rule. One day there was almost a free-for-all between the vets and Jesse. Jesse wasn't going to do the fighting, but Willie Upshaw came to his rescue along with Lloyd Moseby and a couple of the veteran black players. In 1979 we [rookies] sure as hell were not welcome."

* * * *

Barfield once dropped a ball during a ballgame in Milwaukee. After the game, writers asked him what had happened to the usually sure-handed Jay to cause the defensive lapse. His answer took them aback. "Well," he said, "I was looking up and a UFO flew right across. It was weird. I never saw anything like that in my life." Barfield was shocked when his joking comment made it into the next day's sports section.

* * * *

In the 1984 season, Barfield was platooning in right field with Dave Collins. He was hungry for more playing time and more at-bats. The following year Collins was a member of the Oakland A's and the position was all his. He responded with a great season at the plate, including multiple grand slams, the kind you eat that is. Barfield was addicted to the calorie-packed breakfast offering served at Denny's restaurants. Deciding that more is better, Barfield regularly ordered an extra flapjack. If you're scoring at home, that's two pancakes, two scrambled eggs, two bacon strips, and two sausages. At a cost of under $3.00, that gave him over $40.00 in meal money to spend on Pepto-Bismol. "I get teased about it a lot," he admitted, "but I love the pancakes."

* * * *

Barfield enjoyed his playing days in Toronto. Prior to the 1987 season, he admitted that he and his teammates didn't get as much press coverage as baseball clubs south of the border, but he didn't mind. "That's how it is," he said philosophically. "I don't let it bother me. It doesn't matter if I play in Egypt, I still have a job to do. Personally, I like it in Toronto. It's a great place to raise kids."

He did express some less than enthusiastic thoughts about playing in New York. "I'd get more attention if I played in New York, but I really don't think I'd enjoy living there at all. I mean I'd go if I had to, but I just think it would be hard to play there."

As fate would have it, in April of 1989, Barfield was traded to the New York Yankees for pitcher Al Leiter. He never returned to the hitting form he had known in Toronto, although he did win a second Gold Glove.

MIGUEL BATISTA

Pitcher Miguel Batista's stay in Toronto was a two-year whistle stop on an odyssey through the Majors. He started with the Pittsburgh Pirates before moving on to the Florida Marlins, Chicago Cubs, Montreal Expos, Kansas City Royals, Arizona Diamondbacks, Blue Jays, Arizona (again), Seattle Mariners, Washington Nationals, St. Louis Cardinals, NY Mets, and Atlanta Braves.

Regardless of the clubhouse he was in, Batista was invariably the smartest guy in the room—an intellectual, a renaissance man who loves philosophy. Once in Montreal, he entered the clubhouse with a copy of *Gandhi* in his hand. The head trainer was shocked. "You may be the first player I've seen in 35 years that brought a book in here without pictures in it," he said. Not only does he read poetry and fiction, Batista *writes* poetry and fiction. He's articulate, engaging, and witty. The native of the Dominican Republic didn't play competitive baseball until he was 15 and even today, he is not consumed by it. His dream is to become a criminal lawyer and has penned a novel about the search for a serial killer in Arizona. He writes only in longhand because "Typing is like taking the stars out of the sky."

When Toronto reporters came to the clubhouse seeking quotes, they got no clichés from Miguel. After arriving from the National League, where pitchers still have to take their turn at bat, he was asked if he would miss taking his cuts at the plate.

"My hits are just like comets," he responded. "They come every four years."

Batista cares about things beyond the confines of a ballpark, especially the welfare of his fellow man. He is modest about his philanthropic endeavors. "I'm the type of man who believes that real charity doesn't care if it's tax-deductible or not."

TONY BATISTA

One of the great things about baseball is its infinite nature. Games could theoretically go on forever. And the lines that spread out from home plate toward left and right field could too.

Tony Batista came to Toronto as a replacement for injured infielder Alex Gonzalez. In an apparent effort to check out the infinity theory during a 1999 game against the Baltimore Orioles at SkyDome, Batista went to the wall. Obviously the shortstop didn't go there in pursuit of a fly ball, nor did he hit a ball out there. In fact he barely legged out an infield single. And then, apparently deciding that he needed some exercise or as a philosophical journey of baseball discovery, he continued past first base and proceeded to the distant right field wall, a 328-foot jog. On his triumphant return to first base he was greeted with a level of cheering that would have warmed the heart of Olympian Donovan Bailey. Batista was obviously paying attention when his coaches taught him to run out every hit ball.

JOSE BAUTISTA

Interestica

At times, Jose Bautista can be his own worst enemy. The slugger has earned the "whiner" label and gets few close calls from the sometimes-sensitive, sometimes-vengeful umpiring fraternity. He tends to openly challenge balls and strike calls, calling attention to the arbiters and getting the crowd against them.

"I think in Jose's case he's a very good player who could be better. He's shown great leadership qualities but his abilities to rein it in emotionally have been difficult for him with umpires.

I think he has to get better in that category in order to help his teammates and become the team leader that he's capable of," Jerry Howarth noted.

Even Bautista's response to the charges wasn't likely to get him on any Christmas card lists. "Sometimes I have trouble more than other players dealing with my production being affected by somebody else's mediocrity," said the right fielder. "If that's my weakness as a player then I must be doing all right in other aspects."

* * * *

When the Dominican Republic won the 2013 World Baseball Classic, few teams had more reason to celebrate than the Toronto Blue Jays. The Jays had eight Dominicans on the roster on Opening Day, including several star players. The names include Jose Bautista, Edwin Encarnacion, Melky Cabrera, and Jose Reyes.

The Jays' Dominican connection goes way back and includes such stand-outs as George Bell, Alfredo Griffin, Tony Fernandez, Juan Guzman, Junior Felix, and Damaso Garcia.

Of course, it is more than coincidence. The Jays maintain a baseball camp in the shortstop haven of San Pedro de Macoris, a baseball-crazy town in this nation of 10 million baseball-crazy citizens.

* * * *

All that was missing was an iceberg or two and the smell of salt air. It was US Cellular Field, but it looked more like the Grand Banks of Newfoundland. It was Monday, May 10, 2013, and the Blue Jays were playing the White Sox on the South Side of the Windy City, a.k.a. the foggy city. The fog was so thick that Adam Dunn's third-inning home run was little more than a rumor to most fans in attendance. Given the murky surroundings, the ump could just as well have shouted "Weigh anchor!" as "Play ball!"

At the plate, both teams responded amazingly well, although for the hometown White Sox, the prospect of batting against a Cy Young Award winning knuckleballer like R. A. Dickey, in a fog so thick that the game had to be halted for over an hour, must have been daunting.

But Dickey's knuckler didn't fool many people of this bizarre day. Sox slugger Adam Dunn hit two tremendous shots off him into the gloaming.

Nevertheless, Jose Bautista kept the Jays in the game, playing like there was nothing but clear blue skies above. With a man aboard in the first, he hit the first pitch he saw over the fence to stake the Jays to a 2-0 lead. He homered again in the fourth with two men on to stake the Jays to a 5-4 advantage. On a day when others saw little, Bautista's vision was just fine.

"I've been seeing the ball better the last couple days and took advantage of a couple balls right over the heart of the plate," he said.

Unfortunately for the Jays, they ended up on the losing end of the 10-6 spectacle.

* * * *

Riding the coattails of a sartorial triple play, Jose Bautista broke from a prolonged slump by crunching two home runs, including his 200th as he led the Jays to a 6-2 win over the first place Red Sox. It was Saturday, June 29, 2013, but it could have been declared Joey Bats Day in Boston and few would have disagreed. In addition to the pair of homers and three RBIs, the right fielder made a perfect peg from the outfield to nail Red Sox runner Shane Victorino at the plate. He also made a heads-up base-running move that led to Toronto's first run.

Why the sudden success? Baseball players are a superstitious lot and, stuck in the hitting doldrums, Bautista decided to shake things up a bit. Thus he donned R. A. Dickey's pants, wore his socks in the old-fashioned high-cut manner, and returned to his trusty two-tone bat. The change was immediate, like Clark Kent emerging from the phone booth (remember those?) as Superman. Bautista was quick to acknowledge the theory that clothing made the man ... hit two homers. "There's going to be a lot of people suggesting stuff like [that] made a difference," he told reporters after the game. He let the comment, or non-comment, hang in the air like the curveball he had hit out for # 200.

PAUL BEESTON

Toronto Blue Jays president and CEO Paul Beeston was once a diehard Detroit Tigers fan. His father used to take him on annual summer pilgrimages from their Welland, Ontario, home to Briggs Stadium in Motown. "My father could always guarantee we would be behind a pole," he told Jason Winders for the University of Western Ontario Alumni magazine. But while his view of the field may have been obstructed, his larger vision for the game was not. And even though he has brought that vision to reality in the city of Toronto, he admits to still checking out the Tigers' scores every morning.

"That's the funny thing about baseball. Your team is your team. You can move in any other sport and you'll adopt the team from the city you moved to. But you never lose that first team you went for in baseball. It's one of those allegiances. You'll never get into their hearts."

Beeston holds the distinction of being the very first Blue Jay hire, the ground zero of a franchise that has won two World Series championships and several trips to the postseason. After graduating from UWO, the former accountant found a way to combine his love of numbers with his love for the game. After an initial plan to lure the San Francisco Giant north to Toronto collapsed, he became part of the group that was granted an expansion franchise, the first American League team outside of the United States.

"Effective that day, I retired. Every day since has been a Saturday for me," Beeston has said.

* * * *

"Winning and losing, it didn't really matter at that time. I cannot help but think if we won 54 out of 162 games today, that's one in three, it would be the worst season of your life. For us, it was incredibly exciting," Beeston says.

* * * *

Beeston has seen amazing growth on and off the field in his years at the helm of the Blue Jays. When they started in 1977 at Exhibition Stadium he recalls that only 18 games were televised, "We almost had to pay the networks to get our games on TV. And we didn't just play in the worst stadium in baseball. We played in the worst stadium in all of sports."

That all changed in the mid-eighties as the team became first competitive and then dominant, not only on the field but at the box office. By 1993 the team was boasting four million fans per season, best in all of Major League Baseball, and now all 162 games are broadcast coast to coast.

* * * *

Those who think the Blue Jays may want to leave the highly competitive American League East for another division would be wrong. The presence of New York and Boston may make it the toughest place to win, but it also brings in the fans. "I don't care what division we get moved into, as long as the Yankees and Red Sox come with us!" says Beeston.

DEREK BELL

Fans are the Blue Jays biggest asset and the team officially recognizes the fact once a year on Fan Appreciation Day. In 1992, the Jays announced that they would be giving a brand new vehicle to one lucky fan in attendance at the SkyDome.

As the Blue Jays and their fans watched, a Jeep truck drove onto the field from an access door in the outfield. As it made its way toward the infield for the ceremony, there was a polite round of applause and the Blue Jays players—all but one, that is—joined in. Rookie Derek Bell thought the emerald green vehicle looked kind of familiar. He did a slow double-take and then stared wide-eyed, mouth hanging open in hilarious disbelief. Bell looked around to see if anyone else saw anything out of order, but his teammates, notably Kelly Gruber who stood next to him, remained stone-faced. The PA announcer intoned that the winner of the Jeep was seated in Seat 1, Row 7. If it's possible to see inside another person's head, the TV audience got a good view inside Bell's on this day. You can see the wheels turning and the gears grinding. *Could it be? Naw! And yet…*

As the truck grew closer, the guy behind the wheel and his passenger looked kind of familiar too. Yes, he could see now. The driver was Joe Carter, and riding shotgun was Dave Winfield. And, yes, it was his car! They were about to give away the poor rookie's only means of transportation in front of a capacity crowd and a national TV audience. It was almost certainly the most daring car heist in history.

Finally, after the longest double-take in recorded baseball history, Bell's face melted into a smile as he realized he'd been had. A rookie joke that had the entire dugout shaking with laughter.

GEORGE (JORGE) BELL

If you relied on the media reports, you'd think his middle name was George, his first being Temperamental, as in Temperamental George Bell. There is no denying that George Bell was as tempestuous as he was talented. The native of the Dominican Republic was selected by the Blue Jays in the 1980 draft, and in 1984 became part of one of the best offensive outfields in baseball. Playing alongside Lloyd Moseby in center and Jesse Barfield in right, the left fielder helped lead the Jays to their first AL East title the following season.

"I loved George Bell, loved his competitive nature," Jerry Howarth said. "He was one of the best two-strike hitters ever to put on a Blue Jays uniform, worked as hard as he could in left field, had average skills out there but his bat was second to none. MVP in the league back in 1987, helped the Blue Jays considerably with his talent and gain; he was someone who just wanted to win. He was never concerned about individual statistics. It was 'Can the Blue Jays win this game, and how can I help?'"

* * * *

The positive side of the coin was his intensity. He had a burning desire to win. In 1987, his fourth full season, the 28-year-old became the first Dominican selected as the American League MVP. And no wonder. He hit 47 homers and led the AL in RBI with 134—16 of which were game-winners.

* * * *

The Jays picked up George Bell for $25,000 when he was left unprotected by the Philadelphia Phillies in the 1980 Major League draft of minor leaguers. "That," said Epy Guerrero, then director of Latin American scouting for the Blue Jays, "might have been the draft of the century." Guerrero has witnessed Bell taking batting practice in San Pedro de Macoris Stadium. "I saw George hit 50 balls out of the park, one after another," he said later. He didn't take long to tell GM Pat Gillick about the young talent. The Phillies had left Bell unprotected because they mistakenly believed him to be injured and therefore safe from being grabbed. They were wrong.

* * * *

By 1987, the right-handed slugger had evolved into a bona fide hitting sensation, batting .308 with 47 homers and 134 RBI. That same year he boasted a .608 slugging percentage and captured the league MVP Award. The following season he had the kind of start that hitters dream of, powering three home runs off Kansas City ace Bret Saberhagen on Opening Day. Obviously he couldn't maintain that pace and the rest of his season is better remembered for conflicts with then-manager Jimy Williams. When he was put in the lineup as a DH, he went ballistic, throwing a broken bat into the crowd. When he was lifted for a pinch runner he kicked his helmet toward the dugout. Obviously caught up in the spirit of things, Jimy Williams destroyed it with a bat.

* * * *

Bell's eye-popping offense was often not enough to offset the defensive liabilities he brought to the team. Indeed, late in his career, he would fill the DH role for which he was much better suited. Blue Jays fans loved his free-swinging power, but lost patience with his glaring defensive lapses. Boo-birds soon let him know in no uncertain terms that such gaffes were unacceptable. But George did not take criticism well. Following a game on July 5, 1989, in which he had been heckled for an especially egregious pair of errors, he suggested through the media that the "bleeping Canadian fans" could "kiss my purple butt."

The following day a banner in the left field stands proclaimed: GEORGE, WE'RE BEHIND YOU ALL THE WAY.

* * * *

In September of 1987, Detroit Tigers manager Sparky Anderson summed up George Bell's incredible MVP season: "I hear he has a bad shoulder. I wouldn't doubt he damaged it carrying his team."

* * * *

Even the great Ted Williams was impressed with George Bell. Asked in 1988 who was the best hitter in the game, he had this to say: "The best hitter is the most productive hitter—the guy who got the most total bases. Right now that man is George Bell. Bell is a powerful hitter, a strong looking hitter. Every time he makes that connection, it's four bases—and he gets up a lot of times, walks a lot. Mister Bell had 369 total bases last season."

A few years later, Ted had cooled dramatically on Bell. "[Some hitters] are so damn dumb about what's going on. Before long the pitching fraternity catches on and it's all over. They start to go downhill instead of learning and improving. There are dozens of examples to draw from, guys like George Bell. He started out like gangbusters but didn't progress. After awhile he just left me cold. I wouldn't have had him on my ballclub."

* * * *

Bell had his softhearted side. He is famous for his generosity at home in his native Dominican Republic. He also had a disarming—if somewhat offbeat—sense of humor. Once when a group of relatives were in the crowd, he said that he could hear them calling to him throughout the game. A reporter asked what they called to him. "They called me George, man. What do you think?" In 1986, Bell decided to embrace the Canadian winter and try his hand at skiing. He even took a picture of himself on skis and sent it to then–V-P of Business Paul Beeston. The inscription read: "Skiing has been berry, berry good to me. Who needs baseball?"

* * * *

When the Jays played the Yankees at Yankee Stadium in late June of 1987, fans draped a Dominican Republic flag over the center field railing to show their support of Bell and the three other Dominicans on the Jays. Security guards promptly removed it, prompting a minor scuffle. Bell took it in stride, apparently having mellowed since the 1985 playoffs when he was quoted as saying that umpires don't like Canadians and Dominicans.

Emilio Bonifacio

Utility, thy name is Emilio Bonifacio. Bonifacio came to the Blue Jays as part of the blockbuster trade with the Florida Marlins in the off-season prior to the 2013 campaign. In a group that included Josh Johnson, Jose Reyes, and Mark Buehrle, he got little of the media attention.

There was no leisurely home run trot involved in Bonifacio's first Major League dinger. Playing third base for the Marlins against the Washington Nationals on Opening Day of 2009, he hit the ball to the farthest reaches of the ballpark and then raced around the bases for an inside-the-park homer. It was the first time in over forty years that an inside the park homer had been struck on Opening Day.

* * * *

Bonifacio came to the Jays from Miami as a bona fide second baseman, but the season opener can only be described as a disaster. Emilio not only struck out four times to earn baseball's highly uncoveted "golden sombrero," but also he committed three errors in the field. The miscues were key elements in the 6-4 loss to their AL East rival Red Sox. The offensive and defensive nadir for Bonifacio left the media scrambling for words to describe it. Some called it a "hat trick" of miscues. The Red Sox TV announcers Jerry Remy and Don Orsillo hit upon "bonafiasco," and even the most loyal Jays fan would be hard-pressed to disagree. "Boni had a tough night out there," manager John Gibbons said after the game. "But you know, he nearly won the game for us [Thursday] with his defense. But he'll be fine. One thing about him: he shows up to play every day. He'll get through it." In fairness, Bonifacio's experience at second base was limited. He had played the position only 15 games the previous season and had never done so on artificial turf.

Nova Scotia baseball fan Troy Blades points out that "if you play Fantasy Baseball and listen to the Fantasy Focus podcast on ESPN with Matthew Berry, they have a skit where they ask if an up-and-coming player is Bonafide or Bonafacio. "That performance was certainly not bona fide," said Blades.

In sharp contrast to Bonifacio's performance that day was the offensive show put on by Jose Reyes. Reyes went 4-for-5 and homered in the 7th to tie the game before the Red Sox finally came out on top.

* * * *

Pat Borders

"Whenever you would ask Pat about something that happened during the game he would always immediately turn the attention to the pitcher or pitchers he caught that day," Jerry Howarth said. "I remember one day after the Blue Jays won the World series in '92, flying back from Atlanta and one of my sons, Joe, asked him to sign his hat and he did and then Joe asked him if he could put on there World Series MVP and Pat said I really can't do that Joe because there were so many World Series MVPs on this team this year. Now that's humility."

* * * *

Pat Borders just plain looked tough. Not in a muscle-bound Arnold Schwarzenegger way, more in a young Clint Eastwood in *The Good, the Bad and the Ugly* way. He was not particularly big or burly. At a rangy 6'2", 190 pounds, he was certainly not the prototypical (think Yogi Berra or Thurman Munson) square-bodied catcher. In fact he was drafted as a third baseman and had been a quarterback in high school. But tough. And fearless. Base runners rounding third and barreling toward home must have thought that scoring against this guy would be a cake-walk. Tough-as-nails Kirk Gibson tried and failed. Enormous Frank Thomas also tried and failed. The applause was raucous, although Borders missed it, what with being knocked uncon-scious and all. You've heard of Doctors Without Borders? Well, this was a case of Borders without doctors. Later in an interview with Buck Martinez, he downplayed the collision. "I just swal-lowed my chaw and got a little woozy."

* * * *

On a team with a galaxy of stars—including Joe Carter, Roberto Alomar, and Dave Winfield—Borders emerged as the MVP of the 1992 World Series. In the Series-opening loss to the Atlanta Braves in Atlanta, he went 2-for-3. In Game Two, a game in which the Canadian flag was incidentally flown upside down, he got another hit, a double, as the Jays came out on top, 5-4. Back in Toronto, he added another base hit to help the Jays go up two games to one. In the third inning of Game Four, the left-handed-hitting Borders homered to left off Braves southpaw Tom Glavine to stake the Jays to a 1-0 lead. The Jays won again 2-1, and now led the series three games to one. Game Five brought everyone back to earth. Despite having ace Jack Morris on the mound, the Braves treated the game like it was batting practice. The final score was 7-2 for the Braves, but Borders added two more hits— off the always tough John Smoltz—and drove in both Jays runs. He was now hitting .438 in the Series.

It was only fitting that in Game Six Borders got two more hits and drew a walk as the Jays captured their first World Series with a 4-3 win. He would be the only Jays player to get on base via the bat in every Series game, ending up with a .450 average (9 for 20), best by far among Toronto hitters. In fact, the only negative in Border's World Series resume was allowing 15 steals. However, in the seventh inning, with David Wells on the mound, he threw out Atlanta base runner Otis Nixon to quell a potential uprising by the Braves.

Borders was also the only guy to catch a Toronto no-hitter, working the battery with Dave Stieb on September 2, 1990. Oh yes, he also has an Olympic Gold medal from the 2000 Melbourne Games.

RICK BOSETTI

Rick Bosetti joined the Blue Jays in 1978, their second year of existence. Batting leadoff, he hit .249 with 5 homers. Although scarcely Ruthian numbers, he did earn consideration for top rookie.

* * * *

In April of 1979, victories were hard to come by for the fledgling Jays. In six games between April 22-28, the only win came on a 2-0 one-hitter authored by Dave Lemanczyk. Fans had to get their joy from individual accomplishments, and Bosetti provided one during that dry stretch. He went 5 for 5 in front of an appreciative home crowd at Exhibition Stadium. Unfortunately, there was a game the next day as well and Bosetti did something even more impressive, albeit in a negative fashion. He singled into a double play.

The bases were loaded with one out when he stepped to the plate in the game against the Milwaukee Brewers. He singled to drive in the 8th Jays run; however, he got a bit too greedy and decided to stretch the single into a double. The problem was that another Jay, Rick Cerone, was already occupying second base. When the dust had cleared from the rundowns, the third out had been recorded and a scoring opportunity squandered.

* * * *

The dream of every Major League ballplayer is to leave his mark on the game. Ted Williams wanted to be the greatest hitter who ever lived and practiced every day until his hands bled to make it happen. Hall of Fame southpaw Sandy Koufax worked countless hours to perfect the curveball that made his blazing fastball even more unhittable. Brooks Robinson fielded thousands of practice ground balls in order to become a Gold Glove third baseman.

And then there was Rick Bosetti. As goals go, this center fielder aimed much, much lower. His stated goal was to pee on every outfield in the Majors. A man has to have dreams and his were equal parts inspiration and urination.

During his stay in Toronto, he made his quest public. "I've gotten all the American League parks," he proudly admitted. "That's why I want interleague play. To water that beautiful grass in Wrigley Field would be a dream come true." That year he also topped all American League outfielders in putouts, assists and errors.

Too bad the award for top "reliever" goes to a pitcher. He would have led in that category too.

* * * *

Teammate Paul Hodgson remembers the Bosetti legend. "He never wore a cup and he claimed that he had a way of standing in the outfield with his hand in his glove covering his crotch in a relaxed position. That's when he did it."

MARK BUEHRLE

When Mark Buehrle was traded from the basement-dwelling Miami Mariners to the potential penthouse that was the 2013 Toronto Blue Jays, the future looked bright. In fact, Buehrle couldn't wait to get out of Florida where he felt he had been lied to and disrespected.

Buehrle has a reputation of being laid back and doesn't dwell on the past. "I like to have fun on the mound," he told reporters in spring training in 2013. "I'm out there laughing. Good start, bad start, I just throw it out the window and get ready for my next one."

In fact, the only bone he had to pick was a dog-sized one. You see, Buehrle owns a Staffordshire terrier-bulldog mix by the name of Slater, and pit bulls are banned in Ontario. The beloved family pet was rescued from a shelter, where it was slated to be put down. The provincial law forced the Blue Jays pitcher to leave his family—one wife, two kids, and four dogs—behind in St. Louis.

"I don't want to make it a big story all year," Buehrle said at the start of 2013 spring training. "It does suck that my family's not going to be [in Toronto], but guys go through it, guys deal with it. We're going to make it work."

Ironically, Mark's wife Jamie is a passionate defender of pit bulls and an activist against bans of the controversial breed. The pitcher shares her passion for Slater, insisting that he's an ideal pet.

"He's awesome when we have parties at our house," he claims. "Kids run in and ask where Slater is. Every kid wants to go right to him."

* * * *

As love stories go, it may not be Romeo and Juliet. Call it a glove story because Mark Buehrle loves his gloves. So much so that the Jays starter keeps his gamer, and a spare, in a stylish leather bag called the Glove Guardian. The carrying case holds the two Rawlings gloves, and Buehrle takes it with him on every road trip. No, the maker isn't Gucci, it's a company called Tools of Ignorance, cofounded by former Jays catcher John Buck. It would not look out of place in a fashion show.

Many people have warm memories of their first baseball glove. They remember carefully breaking them in and oiling them lovingly. Some youngsters, the author included, may even have slept with their first glove. Buehrle has maintained that intimate relationship through Little League and throughout his major league career. As a result, it may be the most pampered glove since. "I like the Glove Guardian," admitted Buehrle. "I used to have this blue insert that kept the gloves from getting smashed up or crumpled, but this is much better." Indeed, the case has a hard shell that could transport a Faberge Egg without danger of breakage.

"You look at our gloves and most of the time, you forget how much importance we place on them," Buehrle told *Toronto Star* sports reporter Mark Zwolinski. He confessed to spending a considerable part of his 2012 off-season conditioning his new glove for the upcoming season. While many players use fancy conditioners or "folk medicine" concoctions such as shaving cream, his approach is more natural. The process includes playing catch. "It takes a fair amount of time to break in a glove," Buehrle says.

As for his actual *Gold Gloves*, he keeps those at home and is proud of the fact that he was only the third pitcher to win the gilded trophy in each major league.

A. J. BURNETT

Sign of the apocalypse? When injury-prone Blue Jays right-hander A. J. Burnett tore a fingernail off his right index finger, pitching coach Brad Arnsberg reported that he had called in a "nail specialist."

* * * *

Burnett's demeanor on the mound often left him open to criticism. At times it appeared that he just didn't care. Former teammate Matt Stairs is quick to set the record straight: "[A. J.] wanted to win every time out there. He wanted to succeed. We talked a lot and he was one of my favorite guys to talk to and hang around with at the ballpark. He was just that type of happy-go-lucky guy who has fun. He was also a prankster.

"He'd never turn away and not want to pitch. He loved to pitch, always wanted the ball, really enjoyed pitching. It's wrong for people to say he was a guy that didn't care. That's totally wrong. He did have a lot of nagging injuries. Unfortunately there are injuries that are going to happen with a cut of the hand or fingernail or whatever it is. The guy throws a big curveball, so he needs the fingernails."

ROB BUTLER

Rob Butler was the rarest of birds: a Toronto Blue Jay whose natural habitat was actually the city of Toronto. In 1993, he became the first Canadian in almost twenty years to play in a World Series. He was also the first Canadian to win a World Series for a Canadian team. And he has the ring to prove it. Butler debuted with the Blue Jays on June 12, 1993. An injury to his hand suffered trying to steal second limited him to

17 regular-season games. He batted a modest .271 but was eligible for postseason play and contributed a pinch-hit single off Philadelphia Phillies starter Curt Schilling.

MELKY CABRERA

M elky Cabrera signed a two-year, $16 million contract with the Blue Jays on November 19, 2012. The previous season's tests revealed high levels of testosterone, and he subsequently served a 50-game suspension for use of PEDs. Thus, he viewed the move north as a chance for a fresh start in a new league and a new city and a new country.

Melky Cabrera's statement was blunt and to the point. It started with the admission.

"Last season ended for me when I admitted taking a banned substance and accepted and served my punishment of a 50-game suspension."

It continued with the attempt to make amends. *"At the end of last season, when it became clear that I would win the batting title despite my positive test, I asked the Players Association and MLB to make sure a more deserving player won, and I am very happy that my former teammate Buster Posey won that award instead of me."*

And it concluded with a vow: *"I have put my mistakes behind me, have learned my lesson, and have served my punishment. I am here to play the best baseball I can to help the Toronto Blue Jays win a World Championship."*

The next stage was redemption. Cabrera wanted to start his first Blue Jays season with a clean slate. He wanted to be remembered for more than cheating. Unfortunately for the man known as the Melkman, his season soon went sour. His comeback season was marred by injuries, and he played in only 88 games, managing 15 doubles, 3 homers, and a .279 BA. On August 30, he underwent an operation to remove a benign tumor from his lower spine. Fans hope that the Melkman will deliver in coming seasons.

"Melky had a tough year in 2013, and it's hard to comment on him until we see him in 2014 when he's healthy," Jerry Howarth said.

CANUCKS

In total, eighteen Canadians have worn the Blue Jays colors, and they hail from six different provinces. Dave McKay from Vancouver was the first, followed by a brief stint by New Brunswick's Paul Hodgson. Rob Ducey, from Cambridge, Ontario, followed. Then came Montreal's Denis Boucher, Halifax native Vince Horsman, Toronto's own Rob Butler, and Paul Spoljaric from Kelowna, BC. Ontario then gave us reliever Paul Quantrill from Port Hope and Rich Butler from Toronto.

Steve Sinclair and Simon Pond both came from BC and Corey Koskie from Anola, Manitoba. Power hitter and pinch-hit king Matt Stairs came from Fredericton, NB. Scott Richmond came east from North Vancouver and Shawn Hill from nearby Georgetown, Ontario. Surrey, BC, was home to Adam Loewen and Mark Teahen's adopted hometown is St. Mary's Ontario, also home of the Canadian Hall of Fame. Brett Lawrie is a native of Langley, BC.

* * * *

Matt Stairs talked about what it's like to have played for a Canadian franchise:

"I'm proud to have played for a Canadian team. It's quite an honor and would be for any Canadian ballplayer. They would jump at the chance, especially in Toronto where I had a lot of friends from going there as a visiting player. I knew their organization pretty well and I had a chance to meet the majority of them before I signed with the Expos, so it was nice. It's something you'll never forget when you put on that Canadian Blue Jays jersey."

Stairs, a hockey-loving Canadian, compared the work of a baseball player to that of a hockey player:

"Of course as a Canadian I was also a hockey player and I think there is some carryover and transference of skills between the two sports. There are similar assets needed, like good hand-eye coordination. Taking a slap shot and trying to hit a home run involves the same kind of motion with the hips. You don't want to lead too early with your hips to take a slap shot. That's where you generate your power when you take a slap shot and shooting generally—from your hips. It's the same with a baseball. So having developed the strong legs from playing hockey has helped me, given me the drive from the backside for hitting home runs and driving the ball into the gaps."

JESSE CARLSON

Jesse Carlson first took the mound for the Blue Jays on April 10, 2008. It turned out to be a very grand entrance to the major leagues. The Jays were at home to the Oakland Athletics and the two teams were tied after nine innings of play. They were still knotted after 10, and nothing had changed after 11. In the top of the twelfth frame, the A's scored twice off reliever Brandon League, who was sent to the showers with the bases jammed with A's. Carlson came in and struck out Daric Barton to prevent further damage. The Jays lost, but Carlson got kudos for his poise under pressure.

It turned out that this was just the appetizer, because if fans thought he had poise that night, they hadn't seen anything yet. The Texas Rangers came to town just six days later, and again the Jays were in the middle of a nail-biter. The score was even after nine, and both teams went all-out to plate the winning run. In the top of the 11th, Jays pitcher Brian Wolfe had loaded the bases with no one out, and the call once again went out to the young southpaw. With a coolness usually reserved for guys named Mariano Rivera or possibly that ubiquitous Dos Equis pitchman, Carlson completely froze Adam Melhuse on a called third strike. He then struck out Marlon Byrd swinging and dispatched David Murphy the same way. With just 12 pitches, he had mowed down the side with the bases loaded, in extra innings, using a heady mixture of sliders, curveballs, changeups, and less-than-Koufaxian fastballs.

In short, the physically unimpressive 6', 160-pound rookie had de-escalated an offensive threat that seemed inescapable. It was the first time since 1960 that a pitcher had put out a fire of that magnitude in extra innings by strikeouts. And keep in mind that this was his third game ever in the big leagues. That is the stuff of movies and of legend. He also held the Rangers scoreless in the 12th—three up and three down. Showing a flair for the dramatic, he gave up a leadoff double in the 13th and eventually walked the bases full before retiring the side without any damage. He had done his job.

If this were indeed Hollywood, the Jays would have scored in the bottom of the inning to win the game, and Carlson would have been the darling of an entire city. Alas, baseball is a cruel game that writes its own scripts. The game went on until the 15th, with A. J. Burnett taking the loss in a rare relief appearance. Burnett was the ninth Jays pitcher of the day and with runners at first and third, the veteran uncorked a wild pitch that eluded catcher Gregg Zaun, allowing Frank Catalanotto to cross the plate with what turned out to be the winning run. The drama had lasted just short of five hours and there had been many plot twists, but there was no doubt in anyone's mind that the newest cast member had stolen the show.

Carlson later said that the performance showed him he "belonged" in the majors. "It was definitely a good time out there," he said. "That just gave me a lot of confidence ... I would say after that outing, I really felt like I could be here and be successful and get these guys out. I've kind of been running with that ever since."

No matter how you look at it, he had a spectacular major league debut and an even greater encore. His season record was 7-2.

CHRIS CARPENTER

He was a Carpenter who could have helped rebuild the Jays. Instead, file this one under M for Mistake, or O for the One that got away. Carpenter was on the Blue Jays roster from 1997 to 2002. At that point, GM J. P. Ricciardi was in a cost-cutting mode and the future National League Cy Young winner with the St. Louis Cardinals was seen as expendable, especially when he came down with shoulder problems. "They decided to let me go, and I didn't know what was going to happen," Carpenter said. "I was in a sling and I didn't think a whole lot of teams would be interested in a pitcher with a sling on. Fortunately, there was."

JOE CARTER

AP Photo/Elise Amendola

In terms of iconic Canadian sports moments, this one is right up there with Paul Henderson's winning goal in the 1972 Summit Series. For Blue Jays fans the image is hard-wired into their memory: October 23, 1993. Game Six of the World Series against the Philadelphia Phillies, and a jubilant Joe Carter is jumping up and down along the first-base line as if the ground between home plate and first base had somehow been transformed into a long trampoline. His helmet flies off as he rounds first and heads for second. For many fans, the rest of the trip around the bases is remembered in slow motion. Rounding third and bounding toward home, where he is swallowed up in a throng of back-slapping, high-fiving Blue Jays players and coaches. The fans go berserk with the realization that Carter had just brought Toronto its second World Championship in as many years.

After the Blue Jays made history in 1992 by becoming the first Canadian team to win the World Series, it was felt there would be a let-down. Perfectly understandable. It often happens the year following a championship effort. Not with this group of guys. They were just as hungry in '93 as they had been in '92, and they now possessed a level of confidence that they had not had before.

Rest assured, Carter was never an average Joe. He had always seemed destined to be a hero.

"Joe always had fun playing," Jerry Howarth said. "He lifted his teammates up, had a great sense of humor, and was a dominant player for a decade. He was on winning teams because he was a winner, a huge part of those championship teams. But also was able to see the lightness of it and was able to get people to relax along the way."

* * * *

The significance of the walk-off home run made it much more than a Toronto story. It was a moment that would go down in baseball history as one of the most dramatic World Series finishes ever. Only the 1960 Pittsburgh Pirates, and unlikely home run hero Bill Mazeroski, had done it in such dramatic fashion before. This was the first time the winning homer had also erased a one-run deficit in the bottom of the ninth.

* * * *

The Blue Jays had come close in 1985, 1989, and 1991, only to fall short in the playoffs and disappoint fans across Canada. The 1992 Jays were determined to peel off the "Blew Jays" label that had been attached to them. Joe Carter spoke for the entire team when he was asked about this dismal history. "To hell with history," he said as teachers throughout Canada cringed.

* * * *

Phillies fans have long memories and three years later, when Carter took the field for the American League side at the 1996 All-Star Game in Philadelphia, he received a round of boos. It was the ultimate tribute and sign of respect from the city that once booed Santa Claus.

* * * *

The Carter home run will go down as a classic moment in Canadian sports history. But there was another such moment. Paul Henderson scored the winning goal in the 1972 Summit Series between the Soviet Union and Canada. In fact, he scored the winners in the final three games in Moscow. If you were to hang pictures of Henderson's winning goal and Carter's home run side by side, neither would look out of place. Nor would the TV and radio calls of the events by Foster Hewitt and Tom Cheek, respectively.

Henderson had more than a passing interest in the Blue Jays.

"I used to work with the Blue Jays when Jesse [Barfield], Lloyd [Moseby], Kelly [Gruber], and Tony [Fernandez] were there. We had seven or eight of them that my buddy Gordie Barlow and I we used to do Bible study with. We were a part of that whole thing and had a good time with them."

Not surprisingly, Henderson enjoyed the '93 dramatics. "That was big!" he said. "They were a great team. They had the great pitchers and great hitters—the complete package. I thought they had the best team. They deserved to win it. And Big Joe, he came up big! I can still see him, jumping like a kangaroo around the bases."

So what do two bona fide heroes of Canadian sports history talk about when they meet? "We haven't actually compared notes on the two events," says Paul. "I congratulated him, but mine had happened long before that. He knew that I had scored a big goal, but I can't ever remember talking about it." And how does Henderson compare the two iconic moments? "Obviously I was more involved in the first. This one was strictly as a fan," he said modestly.

* * * *

A year earlier, Carter had also played a major role in the '92 October Classic against the Atlanta Braves. He had socked two homers and registered the final out as reliever Mike Timlin fielded an Otis Nixon bunt and threw to first for the thrilling victory.

* * * *

Although he could hit the ball out of any park including Banff, Carter loved to hit in Fenway Park in Boston. He used to aim for the giant CITGO sign that looms well beyond the famous Green Monster. "It advertises CITGO gas," he explained, "but the first time I looked at the sign, that's what popped into my mind: See it go." Apparently Joe was hooked on phonics.

RICO CARTY

Rico Carty was slow of foot, and his glove was more of an adornment than a defensive tool. He had more maladies than an entire season of *ER*. He endured a bout of full-blown tuberculosis that cost him the 1968 season and threatened his career. When he returned, he suffered back problems, a broken kneecap, and multiple shoulder dislocations.

But Rico Carty could hit, and he did so with gusto, even in the minors. As a member of the Toronto Maple Leafs in the International League, he once hit two homers in a single at-bat. Whaaa? You might well ask. The first home run was hit just after time was called by the home plate umpire. So Carty dug in again and, you guessed it, hit another. This one was put on the scoreboard.

Carty didn't become a Blue Jay until late in his career.

Luckily for him, his career overlapped with the introduction of a new rule that allowed him to concentrate on what he did best—the DH rule. The man known as "Beeg Mon" was the last guy a pitcher wanted to see come to the plate with men on base. Once settled in the batter's box, he was completely focused—no fidgeting, no wasted movement—sometimes not even a practice swing.

Many Ontario residents will remember Rico Carty not only for his on-field exploits as a Toronto Blue Jay but also as the pitch man for car safety belts, an idea that in the late '70s had yet to become popular, let alone mandatory.

FRANK CATALANOTTO

The baby-faced Catalanotto came to Toronto in 2003 from the Texas Rangers. He started out like gangbusters and had five consecutive multiple-hit games by May 1. He finished the season with a .299 batting average, 13 homers, and an impressive 34 doubles.

The following year he ended up on the DL for much of the season. Nevertheless, there were moments of glory. In a 10-6 May 1st victory over the White Sox, he equaled an American League record by rapping out six hits, the first Blue Jay to join that exclusive club. He rebounded from the injuries with two consecutive .300 seasons in 2005 and 2006. In the field he was all but flawless, recording a stretch of 212 games without an error.

* * * *

Catalanotto established the Frank Catalanotto Foundation, an organization "dedicated to raising awareness and aiding with the early intervention of vascular birthmarks." Frank and his wife Barbara started the foundation driven by love for their daughter Morgan. A vascular birthmark (or hemangioma) is a type of vascular anomaly of the skin that, if left untreated, can spread rapidly. Shortly after birth, Morgan's parents identified what turned out to be a vascular birthmark on the face of their newborn.

* * * *

It may not have been the logbook of the Starship Enterprise, but it sure took a lot of enterprise to create it. Of course, every hitter likes to think he has a book on pitchers, but Frank Catalanotto really did. He could often be seen on the bench leafing through a tattered black binder. It was as complete as any diary could be. The binder was the repository of page after page of pitchers' names, all in alphabetical order. After every game, he painstakingly recorded every one of the more than 2500 plate appearances he had in the majors. It was handwritten and detailed. It described every one of the more than 8500 pitches he had thrown to him since he broke in with the Detroit Tigers. It told the reader what the pitch was—fastball, slider, curve, etc.—and the location of the pitch. But it didn't stop there. It also recorded what he had done with every pitch—the homers, the base hits, the strikeouts, etc.

Catalanotto would turn to the appropriate page before every game and review his past at-bats against that day's starter. It enabled him to discover what the pitcher liked to throw in different situations and to pick out patterns that might be otherwise overlooked. If a pitcher showed a subtle change in his delivery—a different arm angle, or even the way he shielded his grip in the glove before the pitch—that information became a vital piece of the puzzle that the hitter was trying to solve. He was telegraphing what he was going to throw, and Catalanotto's book allowed him to crack the code. Knowing that a certain pitch was coming made hitting that pitch a much easier task.

"For example," he told Daniel Habib in 2004, "let's say in the first at-bat against a guy, I see a 2-and-0 changeup outside and I get a base hit to left field. Then the next time he tries to bust me inside, I'll say, *O.K., if I get a hit on something soft and away, the next at-bat he likes to come in hard.* I can see how a guy pitched to me when I had success against him and what the guy did when he got me out. It's homework. I don't have all the talent in the world, so I make up for it by trying to be a smart player."

In the age of Kindles and iPhones, the low-tech approach may seem quaint, but his dedication to the task overcame any such criticisms. His work ethic and study habits would rival any player in the game. He was always first to the ballpark, eager to search the videotape for flaws in his swing and tendencies of that day's pitcher. He would show up at the ballpark a few hours before each game to study videos of the opposing pitcher. Like Ted Williams and other students of the science of hitting, he would consult fellow hitters for advice.

* * * *

After some negotiation, Catalanotto struck a deal with a Toronto newspaper to publish some entries from his book, but only on the condition that they change the names of the pitchers involved. The last thing you want as a hitter is a pitcher who knows that you know what he knows. Better that he doesn't know you know. Or something like that.

BRETT CECIL

When Jays southpaw Brett Cecil first arrived in Toronto he had a 95-mile-an-hour fastball and a "can't-miss" label firmly attached to his spanking new uniform. In 2010, he went 15-7 and enjoyed the number-one spot in the Blue Jays pitching rotation in 2010. In 2011, he fell to 4-11 and was exiled to the far reaches of the bullpen. In 2012, he had ample time to seek answers as he did a tour of the minor leagues. His fastball had dipped below the 90-mile-per-hour mark, making him just another minor league pitcher. He needed a ticket back and found it in early 2013.

"In 2010, I had a kind of a p***k attitude on the mound," Cecil told the *Toronto Sun*'s Bill Lankhof. "Not to say that there was anything bad about the guys I was facing. But they were trying to take my money and the food off my table." As his temper fell, so did the speed of his fastball.

"Baseball is so much a mental thing," he continued. "I think that's kind of the attitude that I lost in 2011 and 2012. Now I feel I've got that back. I'm pitching with more of [a] chip on my shoulder. More attitude. At this level, to pitch, you need to be a jerk."

And it worked. The madder he got, the more velocity his fastball had. Of course he also took a Velocity Training Program, and got some advice from new teammate and fellow pitcher Mark Buehrle.

"He just throws whatever sign the catcher puts down and I've learned from that," he told Lankhof. "He has conviction in every pitch. He hits his spots. It's pitch location and he understands that and it's what I'm trying to do, too. Whether it's 88 mph or 98 mph, it has to be located well. It's why he's so good."

* * * *

Cecil may be a southpaw on the mound, but he's a northpaw in everything else. Throwing a baseball is the only thing he does left-handed. And while it may not be his dominant hand, he can still dominate with it.

It's not unusual for hitters to bat from both sides or even for natural right-handers to bat only from the left side (Ted Williams is a notable example), but it's an oddity in the pitching fraternity.

Morgan Campbell of the *Toronto Star* (May 15, 2009) reported that even Jays pitching coach Brad Arnsberg wasn't aware that Cecil was a rightie. His reaction when he was told? "Obviously, he picked the right hand to throw with."

Cecil's switch to the left dates back to his earliest years, as a three-year-old about to turn four. It was decided that he'd get a baseball glove as a gift. "My mom told my aunt to get me a right-handed glove," Cecil recalled. "So I just used that one." From such misunderstanding, a new southpaw was born.

JOHN CERUTTI

Left-handed John Cerutti served as both a starter and a reliever for the Blue Jays teams of the late 1980s.

Cerutti got the call to join the parent Blue Jays on September 1 of 1985. After his flight, and delays caused by the opening of the CNE, he didn't arrive at the ballpark until the fourth inning. He donned his spotless clean new Jays uniform and made his way to the dugout, where he was welcomed by manager Bobby Cox and some of the Jays players. To Cerutti's considerable surprise, Cox asked if he was ready to pitch. Although he was stunned, he managed to stammer, "Yes, of course."

The Jays' pitcher, Jim Acker, had loaded the bases against the visiting Chicago White Sox. There was no one out, and Cerutti was being asked to come in to face their toughest hitter, Harold Baines. Talk about baptisms of fire. The meeting on the mound was short and sweet. Steve Nicosia was the catcher, having just been acquired from the Montreal Expos. "When I arrived at the mound," Cerutti recalled years later, "Bobby Cox said, 'Welcome to the big leagues, kid. Steve, this is John. John, this is Steve.'" After throwing two pitches well out of the strike zone, Cerutti struck out Baines swinging.

* * * *

On May 25, 1986, Cerutti was involved in a very rare play. The Blue Jays were playing the Indians at the old Cleveland Municipal Stadium. With future Jay Pat Tabler at the plate for the Indians, and future Jay Joe Carter on first, Cerutti picked Carter off first base unassisted by outracing him back to the bag. He was ready to face the always-tough Carlton Fisk when he saw Cox making his way to the mound. Cox called in Bill Caudill and Cerutti's first major league appearance was over. As he left the mound, the warm applause of the fans washed over him. "I was thinking, *I have struck out everyone I have faced in the big leagues and they are taking me out of the game.*"

* * * *

The John Cerutti story has a sad ending. When his playing days were over, the articulate southpaw pursued a broadcasting career, initially working Blue Jays games with Brian Williams at CBC. He then moved on to Rogers Sportsnet as a TV analyst. He was scheduled to broadcast the final game of the 2004 season but failed to show up for the pregame meeting. After several failed attempts to contact him, police went to his hotel and forced open the door to his room. The pitcher had died of heart arrhythmia at the age of 44. Later that year, he was awarded the Good Guy Award by the Toronto chapter of the Baseball Writers Association of America. The award is presented to the person who "best exemplifies a positive image for baseball." No one could be more deserving.

Tom Cheek

For Blue Jays fans who followed the team from the very first pitch of 1977 until his last call on April 4, 2005, Tom Cheek was not only the voice of the Blue Jays, but also he was the beating heart of the Jays. Fans followed him—imprinted on him like baby ducks on their mother. His epic call in the 1993 World Series, "Touch 'em all Joe. You'll never hit a bigger home run in your life!" will live forever in Canadian sports lore.

Cheek's first broadcast partner was Early "Gus" Wynn, a former pitcher with more than 300 wins under his belt. While the pair was working a Jays night game in Texas, a pop-up came within range of a young couple near the fence down the second base line. The young man made a valiant effort and managed to get his hands on the ball, but dropped it. He was treated to a chorus of boos from the fans in the vicinity. During the same at-bat, another foul pop came his way and the young man, thinking to redeem himself in the eyes of the fans and his girl-friend, lunged for the ball. Before he could corral it, the young lady made an impressive one-hand catch, receiving a burst of applause from the crowd.

Tom Cheek was impressed. "Can you believe it?" he said. "He boots it and she catches it. How about that!?" To which his partner, Early Wynn, replied, "Well, she probably knows all about his hands."

* * * *

From 1980 until 2004, he was paired with Gerry Howarth to form the famous Tom and Gerry team that was a mainstay for fans up until Cheek's passing. Listening to these down-to-earth professionals was like having two old friends drop by to discuss baseball.

It's not easy to cover a team that finishes last in their five sea-sons of existence. But it does sharpen the wit and the art of story-telling. When the years in the baseball wilderness were blessedly past, he shone even brighter, taking the long-suffering fans along on the ride and making them feel a part of it.

In 1992, Cheek officially became what we all considered him to be anyway—a Canadian citizen.

JIM CLANCY

J im Clancy was a charter member of the Toronto Blue Jays and played for them from 1977 to 1988 before moving on to Houston and then Atlanta. The mustachioed 6'4", 220-pound right-hander featured a fastball, slider, occasional forkball, straight changeup, and a slow curve.

When Clancy first arrived at Exhibition Stadium after being snatched from Texas in the expansion draft, he saw no problem with the oft-criticized ballpark. "I'd been told it was like a minor league park," he recalled. "But all I was used to were minor league parks, and it felt more major to me."

Years later, Clancy still remembered his first big-league starting assignment. He lasted only two innings in a 15-5 shellacking at the hands of the Texas Rangers. He also recalled a 1977 game at Exhibition Stadium against the visiting Baltimore Orioles and their fiery little general, Earl Weaver. Clancy got an easy win, as Weaver pulled his team off the field, complaining that the tarps placed over the bullpen mounds were a safety risk for outfielders. Weaver probably had a solid point. The tarps that covered the mounds were held down with concrete blocks. It went into the record books as a 9-0 victory for the Jays.

* * * *

Clancy was on the mound when the Blue Jays turned the first triple play in franchise history. On April 22, 1978, a full house was on hand at Exhibition Stadium to see the Jays play the Chicago White Sox. With no one aboard in the top of the second inning, Bobby Bonds lowered the boom on Clancy, hitting a fastball for a home run. Lamar Johnson then doubled to left but was unable to advance when Ron Blomberg legged out an infield single. The next batter was Junior Moore and the Jays infield was expecting a bunt. Sure enough, Moore squared to bunt the ball but popped it up. Clancy caught the ball and threw a laser to first to retire Blomberg, who was stuck in no man's land between first and second. First baseman John Mayberry pivoted quickly and threw to shortstop Luis Gomez, who was covering second.

* * * *

On September 28, 1982, Clancy flirted with perfection in the first half of a doubleheader against the Minnesota Twins. Inning after inning, Clancy used his blazing fastball and an elusive slider to mow down the Twins. The modest Exhibition Stadium crowd hung on every pitch and no one in the Jays dugout uttered a syllable about what was happening on the field. Eight innings and 24 straight outs left him just three outs from that rarest of pitching feats. "By the ninth my knees were shaking," he admitted years later. "I didn't want to walk anybody." But, alas, it was not to be. Randy Bush hit a modest, broken-bat flair over second and the gem was tarnished beyond repair. "My heart just sank," said Clancy. "I've still got the ball at home."

* * * *

Clancy's usual battery mate throughout his tenure with the Blue Jays was Ernie Whitt. On one famous occasion while Clancy was in the clubhouse toilet, Whitt dumped a bucket of cold water over the partition and onto Clancy's head. A few days later Clancy retaliated by cutting the legs off his catcher's pants. He then taped them back together with clear tape and hoped that they would separate at a most inopportune moment.

ROGER CLEMENS

It was one of the most notable free agency acquisitions in history. After spending the first 13 seasons of his major league career as a member of the Boston Red Sox, in December of 1996 Clemens became a Toronto Blue Jay, signing a $40 million deal over four years.

Once the best pitcher in the game, Clemens had struggled in his final four seasons in Boston. In 1993 his record was 11-14 with a 4.46 ERA; in '94 he was 9-7, 2.85; in '95 he was 10-5, 4.18; and in '96 he was 10-13 with a 3.63 ERA. When he left the Red Sox, GM Dan Duquette's parting words were, "We had hoped to keep him in Boston during the twilight of his career." Those were fighting words to the Rocket.

And then came Toronto, where Clemens pitched as if he had consumed a magic elixir. Despite pitching only two seasons for the Jays, the statistics that he rang up in those two seasons were four-year's worth for many starters. In his first season north of the border, he had a record of 21-7 with a microscopic ERA of 2.05 and 292 strikeouts and won the Cy Young and the pitching triple crown (Wins, ERA, and strikeouts). The Jays finished dead-last that season, making his accomplishment even more unbelievable. As an encore the following year, he went an astounding 20-6 with a 2.65 ERA and 271 whiffs and captured a second Cy Young and second triple crown. That year he helped the Jays improve slightly as they climbed the ladder to third place. His record during that incredible stretch of pitching excellence was 41-13 and his ERA was a combined 2.33. Posting numbers like these on a non-contending club was miraculous.

* * * *

It is arguably impossible to talk about Roger Clemens without discussing the steroid scandal that plagued the sport throughout the second half of his career. It's as if his name may be destined to appear with an asterisk next to it, if not in fact, at least in many people's minds.

In Red Sox fan Bill Simmons's May 29, 2001, *Page 2* column entitled "Is Clemens the Anti-Christ?" the author outlines the many knocks on the fastball pitcher.

"Anyway, we watched in horror as Clemens rolled off *consecutive Cy Young seasons* for the Blue Jays. Here were his average stats from '93-'96 in Boston, followed by the '97 and '98 seasons in Toronto:

YR	W-L	ERA	G	IP	H	SO	BB
93-96	10-10	3.90	26	186.1	164	204	76
1997	21-7	2.05	34	264.0	204	292	68
1998	20-6	2.65	33	234.2	169	271	88

Put it this way: Watching Clemens lighting it up in Canada was like breaking up with your girlfriend, then watching her hire a personal trainer, shed 15 pounds, spend 10 Gs on a boob job and join the cast of *Baywatch*." It didn't help that Clemens was lights-out against the Red Sox.

* * * *

Many Jays fans eventually had a similar attitude when Clemens moved his act to New York to become a Yankee. His departure from Toronto was no more gracious than the one that took him from Boston to Toronto. The first time he was shopped around he had turned down the Yankees in favor of Toronto, citing a desire to raise his kids in a better environment. Of course the four-year deal for over $31 million didn't hurt either. This time, he couldn't wait to take a bite out of the Big Apple. "I made a mistake once," he said, "but hopefully not twice." This kind of talk did not endear him to Jays fans. As for the Yankees, New York general manager Brian Cashman admitted that when he got the call from Jays GM Gord Ash with the offer of Clemens for Wells, Bush, and Lloyd "it made my knees buckle."

DAVE COLLINS

Dave Collins was deceptive. He did not look like a speedster. One writer called him a "slightly cooler version of Rick Moranis."

But when he got on the base paths, he morphed from your father's '84 Oldsmobile into a Ferrari. In 1984, Damaso Garcia stole 46 bases for the Jays. Lloyd Mosby added another 39. And yet it was deceptive Dave who gave opposing American League pitchers the worst nightmares. In 1984, Collins stole 60 bases, still a Blue Jays team record almost thirty years later. Batting second in the lineup ahead of sluggers Bell and Barfield, he was also a highly efficient thief, succeeding on 81 percent of his attempts that season. But his speed didn't stop there. He also recorded a league-leading 15 triples while batting .308. His success rate in taking the extra base was 53 percent.

DAVID CONE

David Cone made two stops in Toronto in his long and illustrious Major League career. The first came in 1992 when the Jays, who were battling for the American League, sent Jeff Kent and Ryan Thompson to the NY Mets in a mid-season swap. The Jays needed a reliable fifth starter and Cone stepped in and gave them 7 starts and a short relief stint down the stretch. His record was 4-3 on the strength of a superb 2.55 ERA. He also added 47 strikeouts to go along with the 214 whiffs he recorded as a Met (261 overall). His strikeouts led the major leagues that season and were a career high. He was tabbed to start two games in the ALCS against Oakland. In Game Two, the wily veteran struck out Rickey Henderson on three pitches to start the game and then scattered five hits and allowed a single run in a 3-1 victory at SkyDome to even the series at 1-1. One writer described Cone as looking like a Las Vegas blackjack dealer, as he dealt an assortment of sliders, split-finger fastballs, and fastballs to the befuddled A's. His fans called themselves Coneheads and they were out in full force, sporting the pointed, flesh-colored skull caps to resemble the Conehead family of *SNL* fame. Even Jays pitchers Duane Ward, Mike Timlin, and David Wells were spotted wearing them in the bullpen.

Cone tried to reprise his act in Game Five in Oakland, but the A's didn't cooperate. Rickey Henderson proved especially uncooperative, running amok on the base paths and scoring 2 runs, while disconcerting Cone and the Jays defense. Working on just three days rest, Cone gave up six runs in the 6-2 dismantling.

Fortunately the Jays recovered to win Game Six and punch their ticket to the World Series against the Atlanta Braves. In Game Two of the October Classic, Cone pitched six innings, gave up 4 runs, and came away with a no-decision in the 3-1 loss.

In Game Six, David Cone became a lasting part of Blue Jays history. He started the game and went six strong innings before exiting with a 2-1 lead. Unfortunately, closer Tom Henke could not hold the lead in the ninth and the game proceeded to extra innings. The rest is history, as the Jays won 4-3 in the eleventh. Cone's postseason line was 1 win, 1 loss, and a 3.22 ERA. Oh yes, and a World Series ring.

* * * *

Cone's second tenure in Toronto wasn't nearly as eventful. Reacquired from the Kansas City Royals in 1995, he posted a very respectable 9-5 record with an equally respectable 3.38

ERA. However, the '95 Jays were not contenders and before the season was over, he was dealt to the Yankees.

BOBBY COX

They say that baseball managers are hired to be fired, and even the legendary ones are subject to that baseball truism. Cox was hired by the Atlanta Braves in 1978 and fired by Braves owner Ted Turner in 1981. When Turner was asked who he'd like to hire to replace Cox, he replied, "It would be Bobby Cox if I just hadn't fired him, we need someone like him around here."

If that sounds confusing, it shouldn't be. Every team could benefit from "someone like" Bobby Cox. The Toronto Blue Jays knew that and hired him in advance of the 1982 season. It was a watershed moment in the history of the young franchise. His presence in the dugout brought immediate dividends to the underachieving Jays. Long-suffering fans cheered the Jays as they delivered their first winning season in 1983. Cox remained in Toronto for four years and the Jays got progressively better each year under his reign. In 1984 they rose to second place and seemed poised to rise even further.

In 1985, with stars like George Bell and Tony Fernandez onboard, Cox led the team to 99 wins and a trip to the American League Championship Series, their first-ever postseason appearance. In doing so, he became a kind of Moses of Toronto baseball, leading them from the wilderness of mediocrity to the land of promise and hope. Unfortunately, the Braves, still in need of "someone like" Bobby Cox, saw the error of their ways and lured Cox back to Atlanta as general manager.

* * * *

After a hard-fought June 6, 1984, win over the powerful Detroit Tigers, a reporter commented that Jays pitchers had "handled the meat of the order" well. Cox was in no mood for such talk: "Meat of the order? That's all they've got in their order is meat. Do you see any vegetables? I don't."

* * * *

Lou Pinella? A mere tantrum thrower. Tommy Lasorda? Good style points, but no substance. Billy Martin? Great potential but lacking in longevity. Earl Weaver? Please. During his managerial career Bobby Cox had a better chance of being thrown out of a game than a square baseball, more than any other manager had been in the history of the game. He got the old heave-ho 161 times, many of those premature trips to the showers coming when he was skipper of the Toronto Blue Jays. On one of those occasions—September 25, 1983—he was ejected for throwing a bat from the dugout to protest the umpire's ruling that Dave Stieb had hit A's batter Mike Davis. Cox exited only to return and watch the rest of the game through a crack in the fence behind home plate.

* * * *

While he was still manager of the Jays, Cox once visited the Metro Zoo with his wife Pam. One of the animals in particular captured his attention. "It's those gorillas," his wife told the *Toronto Star*. "He's just mesmerized by them. He could stand there and watch them all day long. I couldn't understand why until he said to me, 'Honey, would you just look at the arms on those guys. Could you imagine our team signing one of them?'"

Rajai Davis

"How'd you like the doubleheader?" That was John Gibbons's reasonable question to reporters after a grueling 18-inning win over the Texas Rangers on June 8, 2013. It was the second time Gibbons had managed the Jays to a win in such a marathon.

It was the kind of game that could make you an instant hero, or put you in an instant slump, as several players discovered. It was the second time in their history that the Jays had extended a game to 18 frames, the other being a July 28, 2005, win over the Angels during Gibbons's first term as manager. Pete Walker, who is now the Jays pitching coach, recorded the win in the 2-1 marathon.

Starter Mark Buehrle was followed by a parade of eight relievers in the 4-3 Jays win. Epic games such as this have heroes and goats, and the unlikely hero of this battle was Rajai Davis, a defensive replacement. Despite coming into the game in the eighth inning, he still ended up playing 10 innings. Davis delivered a two-out base hit past third base in the bottom of the 18th to finally bring the game to a merciful end. "Considering I got in in the eighth and still played a full game, it's pretty remarkable," Davis said after the contest.

Also firmly in the hero category were Adam Lind, who chipped in with four hits, and Colby Rasmus, who tripled in the third inning to plate two runs. Emilio Bonifacio set the stage for Davis's winning hit by rapping a single off Texas reliever Ross Wolfe. The speedy Bonifacio then reached third on Wolfe's errant pickoff attempt that eluded first baseman Lance Berkman.

Instant slump status was imposed on Texas's Jurickson Profar (1-for-7), Adrian Beltre (1-for-8), and Nelson Cruz (0-for-6). For Toronto, Jose Bautista (1-for-8) and Maicer Izturis (0-for-7) were frustrated at the plate. Nevertheless,

Bautista threw Lance Berkman out at home in the 11th. Buehrle pitched well and deserved better, out-pitching the Rangers' much-heralded Yu Darvish. The Jays were in the lead 3-1 when he exited, but usually reliable closer Casey Janssen blew the save in the ninth, forcing extra innings.

In a show of youthful enthusiasm for the game he loved, Cubs legend Ernie Banks once declared, "It's a beautiful day. Let's play two!" It's likely that Banks would have doubly enjoyed this game. And there is no doubt that the crowd of 44,079 got double their money's worth.

* * * *

We can only guess that after the game, Gibbons's lineup card must have resembled the rough draft of *War and Peace*.

* * * *

Meanwhile, as the Rangers and Blue Jays battled through a dozen and a half innings, the New York Mets and Miami Marlins were engaged in their own baseball version of the New York marathon. Columnist and admitted "baseball nerd" Marilee Gallagher compiled some interesting stats on the two games combined. Combined game time: 11 hours and 53 minutes

Total innings: 38
At-bats: 268
Pitches thrown: 1,089
Total # of batters: 65
Combined batting average: .219 (36 for 164)
Pitchers used: 31

The 38 innings that the two games produced is a new major league record. It was also the first time since 1991 that two opposing relievers survived for more than six innings.

STEVE DELABAR

Right-handed pitcher Steve Delabar came to the Blue Jays in exchange for Seattle Mariners outfielder Eric Thames in a July 30, 2012, transaction. It didn't take long for him to make Blue Jays, and baseball, history. His moment came on August 13, 2012, when he struck out four batters in the 10th inning to secure a Jays 3-2 win over the Chicago White Sox. It was the first time a major league pitcher had whiffed four in extra innings. Delabar struck out Dayan Viciedo and then Tyler Flowers swung and missed a 3-2 split-finger fastball for the second strikeout. But the ball eluded catcher Jeff Mathis, and Flowers made it to first base. Delabar then struck out Gordon Beckham on three pitches and Alejandro De Aza on four offerings to establish the record.

* * * *

Here's the unlikely script: A young Steve Delabar is selected in the 29th round of the 2003 draft by the San Diego Padres. Six years later, still toiling in the low minors, he fractures his right, pitching, arm while playing for the Class A Brockton Rox of the Can-Am League.

Delabar was no fool. He knew that there were only two chances of him ever making the majors: slim and none. Then 28 years of age, he decided to get on with his life. That included working as a substitute teacher while completing his university degree. He got his baseball fix through coaching baseball and playing slow-pitch softball.

In the spring of 2011 he started working out, experimenting with a new exercise regimen that he thought might help his students. The results were amazing—so amazing that people started to notice. His strength returned and his pitch velocity increased dramatically. He decided to give pro ball one last try.

A friend contacted Seattle Mariners scout Brian Williams who, strictly as a courtesy, came to see Delabar.

Williams watched Delabar and was impressed, even though he hadn't pitched in more than two seasons, and even then in the low minors.

"The day before, [Williams] called me and said he was coming through the area to go watch a high school kid south of where I live, and he asked if I could throw for him," Delabar told George Chisholm at *MLB.com*. "I was like, 'Ah, my velocity's up, but I don't know if I'm ready.'"

Of course, Delabar desperately needed a catcher and the only one he could think of played for the local high school. "I had to call our local high school catcher, get him out of school, get him some lunch, and then have him meet up with us for the workout," recalled Delabar.

Williams dutifully reported back to the Mariners organization that they may have a sleeper on their hands. They reviewed details from his medical file related to the steel plate that had been inserted into his arm. They were reassured enough to invite him to a more formal workout, this one in Seattle. Again he impressed. The Mariners signed him to a contract. He worked his way up through the system and arrived in the Majors late in 2011.

The fact that the pitcher went from such an unlikely start to an all-star selection—with a first-half 5-1 record and 1.74 ERA—as a member of the Jays boggles the mind. It's not supposed to happen that way.

CARLOS DELGADO

AP Photo/Nick Wass

Carlos Delgado may be the greatest Blue Jay player ever. He's certainly among the classiest and most popular. During his stay in the Queen City from 1993-2004, he was an offensive juggernaut. His batting average over that 12-season span was .282, and prominent among his total of 690 extra base hits were 336 homers. He drove in 1,058 runs and posted a staggering .949 OPS. He is the top Jay in plate appearances (6,018), runs scored (889), slugging percentage (.556), OPS (.949), total bases (2,786), doubles (343), home runs, RBIs and walks (827). He also set the standard in number of times hit-by-pitch (122), extra-base hits (690), and intentional walks (128). In short, by the time he finally moved on the NY Mets, he left behind a record book with his name all over it. Delgado's final career numbers featured a .280 batting average, 473 homers, and an OPS of .929.

"I really liked Carlos and that big bright smile of his," Jerry Howarth said. "He was the home run leader here, did everything well, and had just a great way about him. Everyone enjoyed being around Carlos. He certainly made his mark here and was the only Blue Jay ever to hit four home runs in a game. He definitely stood out among all the Blue Jays that have been here regarding his class and his ability to play the game."

* * * *

Numbers don't lie, and these numbers are impressive: Delgado's home run totals show him to be the all-time leader among players wearing Blue Jays colors.
1. Carlos Delgado 336
2. Vernon Wells 223
3. Joe Carter 203
4. George Bell 202
5. Jesse Barfield 179
6. Lloyd Moseby 149
7. Jose Bautista 142

* * * *

But numbers don't really tell you everything about Carlos Delgado, because if ever the Blue Jays need an ambassador, Carlos should get strong consideration. On the field he was a constant offensive threat. Off the field he conducted himself with poise and class. He was very active in worthy causes within the Toronto community and in his native Puerto Rico, where he was an outspoken humanitarian. Little wonder that he was one of the most respected players in the history of the franchise. Most of the credit must go to his parents, but some also goes to Blue Jays roving instructor Mel Queen, who imparted words of wisdom to the then 17-year-old phenom when he first encountered him in his native Puerto Rico: "Do things right, even when nobody is watching." Delgado took these words to heart and followed them in the world well beyond the diamond.

* * * *

Opposing teams who faced the Blue Jays found the key to winning was as easy as ABC: "Anybody But Carlos." As evidenced by the team-record 128 intentional walks he was issued, pitchers learned to pitch around the 6'3", 235-pound first baseman and take their chances with less talented players in the lineup.

* * * *

He is one of a select group of Blue Jays alumni who have their names featured in the Level of Excellence at the Rogers Centre. Others include Cito Gaston, Tom Cheek, Roberto Alomar, Tony Fernandez, Pat Gillick, Dave Stieb, George Bell, Joe Carter, and Paul Beeston. Delgado may be the only one who could actually hit a ball to the distant façade high above the outfield where the plaques are kept.

* * * *

On September 25, 2003, Carlos Delgado put on a display of power so awesome that he was almost deserving of a seat at the UN. Playing against the Tampa Bay Devil Rays, he hit 4 dingers, driving in six runs in the Jays' 10-8 win.

The first, a 3-run knock, came in the first inning off right-handed starter Jorge Sosa. It was his 300th career home run, making him the 98th player in Major League history to reach that plateau. The ball ricocheted off the Windows restaurant and landed in center field, where it was retrieved for Delgado's growing collection of souvenirs. He then added solo shots to lead off the 4th, 6th, and 8th frames. In the 4th, he touched up Sosa once again. In the 6th, his salvo came off southpaw Joe Kennedy, and the parting shot—a mammoth drive to center field on a 2-2 pitch from right-handed reliever Lance Carter, tied the game 8-8. Delgado flipped his bat away in celebration and trotted, head down, around the bases. "I was pretty fired up. I'm not going to lie to you," Delgado said. "As you can tell with the bat flip. I didn't know what I was doing. I was on Cloud Nine out there and enjoying it." The modest SkyDome crowd of 13,408 stood and cheered and Carlos tipped his hat to acknowledge the applause.

Delgado had reason to celebrate. It was only the fifteenth time that a player had hit 4 homers in a game and the sixth time it had happened in consecutive at-bats. It was the first time the feat had been accomplished by a player with just four official at-bats in the game.

After the game, even Delgado was hard-pressed to explain the offensive outburst. "I can't think of any other way to explain it, it just kind of happened," he said. "It seems like everything you hit goes into the air and goes out. I wish I could do it more often."

Ironically, the big slugger was feeling under the weather before the game and had taken cold medicine and a nap, a formula that seems to have worked well. "It's definitely the best day in my baseball career," he said after the game. The last home run ball was also retrieved and Delgado vowed to give it to his mother.

"It was unbelievable. I'll always remember this," said teammate Vernon Wells. "When he's going good there is no telling what he'll accomplish. It's something I'll never forget."

Added Tampa Bay manager Lou Piniella, "It was a Herculean effort. It's only been done five times in the American League. Delgado is capable of getting into those grooves."

Delgado's former Jays teammate Shawn Green was the last player to strike for a quartet of homers. Green did so for the LA Dodgers a year earlier, on May 2, 2002, against the Milwaukee Brewers.

The big first baseman finished the '03 season with 42 homers and 145 RBI, the most in the majors. He finished second to Alex Rodriguez in the MVP voting.

* * * *

Delgado was not a one-dimensional ballplayer. He was a well-rounded individual who made the most of living in a cosmopolitan city like Toronto. He enjoyed the cultural and artistic scene that it offered. He liked to broaden his horizons through travel—sometimes with friend and teammate Shawn Green. He was also a humanitarian. Perhaps the highest compliment that he has been paid came from Cookie Rojas. "Carlos has the same stature as Roberto Clemente. Roberto always tried to help the Latin players and people, and wanted to leave something behind. He wanted to make people better. Carlos has all the same dignity and that same pride."

* * * *

Nowhere was Delgado's humanity more evident than on the tiny tropical island of Vieques, a few miles off the southeast tip of Puerto Rico. Starting in 1938, the island was used in bombing exercises conducted by the US Navy. The population of some 10,000 people have an extremely high rate of cancer and other illnesses. Delgado has made the island one of his causes, condemning the bombing and offering his celebrity and his own money in efforts to stop it. He teamed with other prominent Puerto Ricans to sponsor an ad in the *New York Times* and *Washington Post*. In the conservative world of pro baseball, this was virtually unheard of, but Delgado was unrepentant.

"If someone was using your backyard as a practice range, dropping bombs, how would you feel?" he argued. "It is wrong. In the States, people think it's not a big deal. They've been doing it for 60 years, and no one seemed to worry about it until a man got killed accidentally. But it was no accident; you're bombing a small island. I will be vocal about that."

Delgado seemed unfazed by potential loss of endorsement income from his outspoken defense of his principles. "If you don't want to give me an endorsement because I say that the government is wrong, I don't give a s---," he said.

R. A. DICKEY

There are baseball heroes and then there are the real-life heroes. Blue Jays ace R. A. Dickey is both. His exploits on the mound speak for themselves. But there are mounds and there are mountains and—figuratively and literally—he has conquered both.

In 2012, in support of a group called Bombay Teen Challenge (BTC), he climbed Mt. Kilimanjaro, raising over $130,000 in donations for the charity. In early 2013, he traveled with his two young daughters, Gabriel, 11, and Lila, 9, to Mumbai, India, to see how the money would be spent. The goal of BTC is to eradicate the scourge of the sex trafficking from this impoverished area of the world. Through Dickey's efforts, they hope to transform a former brothel into a health clinic.

"I want my daughters to share the experience not so much as a gratitude check, but to learn that each of us has a capacity to make a difference in this world, and to see that God's grace makes that possible," he wrote in a *New York Daily News* article. "The breadth of the wickedness is almost too much to bear…"

His incredible trip over, Dickey was about to join his new team, the Toronto Blue Jays. While his knuckleball is anything but straight, his emotional pitches were coming straight from the heart.

* * * *

There are about as many English Lit majors in the Major Leagues as there are tobacco chewers in McGill or Harvard. Like most ballplayers, Dickey's locker includes ample reading material. The difference is that his don't have centerfolds. That, among many other things, makes Dickey stand out. He is eloquent and liberal and thoughtful and extremely intelligent. Dickey is a Christian who doesn't just show it in the superficial ways that some athletes are famous for. He shows it in his actions and his social conscience. His rise to the top of his profession has been as erratic as the pitch that brought him to the top of his profession. In his book, *Wherever I Wind Up: My Quest for Truth, Authenticity and the Perfect Knuckleball,* he tells the story of his life in stark detail, including a childhood that was marred by repeated sexual abuse. The fact that he managed to save his marriage, battle thoughts of suicide, and emerge as a scarred but triumphant survivor are testament to his character. After all that, pitching in big games no longer seems so daunting.

"R. A. Dickey had difficult times as a kid growing up, but by writing his book he was able to get it all out. His overall ability with that knuckleball over the last few years has put him on the map as a significant major league pitcher," Jerry Howarth said.

* * * *

The Blue Jays' acquisition of Dickey before the 2013 baseball season was a tonic for Jays fans across Canada. When he arrived at spring training, all eyes were on the knuckleball specialist and expectations were sky high.

He began his workout regimen by throwing to Jays minor league pitching coordinator Duane Johnson. Despite his best efforts, Johnson was unable to corral the butterfly ball, even when the pitcher warned him it was coming. After several pitches danced past the seemingly handcuffed catcher, Dickey offered a sheepish, "Sorry." Bench coach DeMarlo Hale quickly chimed in. "Don't apologize," he said, obviously delighted that the pitches were so unpredictable.

Dickey once threw four knuckleball pitches in a single inning to tie a Major League record.

* * * *

The only thing that has as much movement as an R. A. Dickey knuckler might be the shaking of batters' heads as they head back to the dugout after striking out. And that movement is much more predictable than the knuckler's. Dickey had scarcely arrived at spring training in 2013 after being traded from the Mets (20-6 with a 2.73 ERA; Cy Young Award), when Blue Jays players were showing their bewilderment. The best description may have come from Mark DeRosa, who likened the ball's flight to that of a "paper airplane coming at you." To complicate matters, he throws the pitch at varying speeds and very occasionally sneaks in a mid-80s fastball. After a steady diet of butterfly pitches, the modest fastball looks positively Nolan Ryanian. He also throws the sinker and a decent changeup, two pitches from his repertoire as a "conventional" pitcher.

For his part, Dickey was pleased to see the reactions from Jays hitters.

"If I see those guys talking or shaking their heads, or saying something to the catcher, I know it's probably moving pretty good. I don't always know what it's doing there closer to the plate. I know how it feels when it leaves my hand. If I see guys ... chuckle to themselves or say something to the umpire going back to the dugout, those are little things I look for to know if it's moving well or not."

Dickey has even suggested that he can somewhat control the ball's movement, something that many other knuckle craftsmen have left to the Fates. "I pick a height and let the ball knuckle," he has said.

* * * *

Beauty is in the eye of the beholder. Same with the knuckleball. It has been called a "freak" pitch, a "fraudulent pitch" and worse. "To the masses, it's a circus pitch," concedes Dickey. But to him it is a thing of beauty, a pitch with a mind and spirit of its own. The former Cy Young winner thinks that every child should throw a knuckleball. "When it leaves your hand, it's up to the world what it's going to do."

* * * *

After a stellar performance for the NL in the 2012 All-Star Game, Dickey made an appearance on the *Dave Letterman Show*. Letterman, a knowledgeable fan, discussed the intricacies of Dickey's signature pitch.

Asked what was the slowest he could throw the knuckler, Dickey replied that he'd thrown one 59 mph and that it was like a Bugs Bunny cartoon where the batter swung at the same pitch three times. The usual difference between his knuckleball and fastball is three mph—he usually throws an 82-mph knuckler and tops out at 85 mph on his "heater." Dave asked if he ever hears batters snicker. "I like it when they snicker," replied Dickey.

* * * *

When the much-hyped former Cy Young winner was introduced to Toronto media in early 2013, he extended a word of caution.

"We're in a honeymoon period right here," he said in response to a reporter who had labeled him "the most inter-esting man in the world." "There's going to be a period where

I'm struggling and it's not going to be so interesting." It didn't take long for his prophecy to come true. In the home opener at Rogers Centre, he was loudly booed by the capacity crowd as he left the mound in the fifth inning after a mediocre performance. In fairness, he probably felt like booing himself after the 13-0 drubbing at the hands of the Red Sox. He allowed eight runs in total. Fellow 2012 Cy Young winner David Price of the Tampa Rays also allowed eight on that same day. It was the first time that baseball's reigning top pitchers had both been greeted in such a fashion to start a new season.

Aside from Dickey's pitching, the biggest story of the day was a three-homer outburst by Red Sox third baseman Will Middlebrooks. The 24-year-old almost had a fourth, but the ball died at the warning track in left. "They must've turned the AC off on me," he said. "I was blowing on it running down the line, but it didn't have enough steam."

* * * *

Dickey refers to his tight-knit group of knuckleball aficionados as his "Jedi Council." It seems that his pitch is so alien, so exotic, so hard for mere mortals to understand, that such a support group is necessary for survival. Indeed when he talks about members of the fraternity, it sounds as if he's referring to an endangered species. "There are probably only eight knuckleballers still alive," he told writer Dan Robson, "so you don't have a lot of people to turn to. So it's just nice to talk to somebody who has walked a mile in your shoes." In addition to Wakefield the group includes Phil Niekro and Charlie Hough. Hough's one-word text message after Dickey won the 2012 Cy Young? "Yahoo!"

* * * *

When R. A. Dickey was introduced to the media, Toronto GM Alex Anthopoulos presented him with his pristine new Jays

home jersey featuring #43. Dickey promptly proceeded to put
it on backwards. "How many people does it take to put on a
uniform?" he ad-libbed.

* * * *

It was baseball's version of the brotherhood of the traveling pants.
The slumping Jose Bautista needed a change and Dickey's pants
were the only ones that would accommodate his powerful legs.
The pants had served Dickey well earlier in the week when he
threw a two-hit shutout against the Tampa Bay Rays. And now
Jose Bautista was wearing them in a June 29, 2013, game with
the Red Sox at Fenway Park, where Bautista hit two home runs
to lead the Jays to a 6-2 win over the first place Sox.

BOBBY DOERR

B obby Doerr is the answer to a great trivia question: Who was
the first person to wear a Blue Jays uniform to be elected to
the Hall of Fame? Yup, it's Doerr. The former Boston Red Sox
second baseman and teammate of Ted Williams was a Blue Jays
hitting coach from 1977 to 1981 and helped countless Jays prospects figure out the intricacies of Major League pitching. Doerr
was inducted into the Hall of Fame in 1986.

ROB DUCEY

T wenty-two-year-old rookie Rob Ducey from Cambridge,
Ontario, was just the third Canadian to wear the Blue Jays'
colors. The first home run of his career was almost lost in the
crowd, so to speak. It came on September 14, 1987, and was

one of a record ten homers hit that day by six different Blue Jays players. Ducey's bomb came in the seventh inning and was the eighth of the day, tying the Major League record. Not bad for a 22-year-old rookie inserted into the lineup to replace Lloyd Moseby, who had earlier contributed his own home run. After the game, Ducey was on Cloud Nine, or was it Cloud Ten? "I'm glad I got it tonight," he told the waiting media. "What will stick in my mind most is the major league record. We'll be in Cooperstown now!"

* * * *

Timing is everything, and Ducey arrived in Toronto at a time of plenty. With George Bell, Devon White, and Lloyd Moseby, the Jays had the best outfield in baseball and trying to crack the lineup was a huge assignment.

* * * *

Ducey's last major league home run came as a member of the Montreal Expos in 2001. It came against the Toronto Blue Jays and was struck off pitcher Chris Carpenter.

EDWIN ENCARNACION

"Edwin's ability to cut down his swing and not chase pitches is impressive. He is turning strikeouts into contact and is driving the curveball the other way. That has led to his increased RBIs and his ability to get runners home from third with less than two outs. His play at first base is of a significantly higher caliber than it was at third base. He's become a very good first baseman as well as the dangerous hitter that he is," Jerry Howarth said.

It's the latest incarnation of Encarnacion. All that Edwin Encarnacion lacked was confidence. Never a strong fielder, the third baseman sometimes let his defense affect his at-bats. Once he settled in as the Jays' DH, he was off and running—and hitting. On June 12, 2012, against the National League's Milwaukee Brewers, he joined Colby Rasmus and Jose Bautista to combine to hit back-to-back-to-back home runs. At the end of the year, he had put up some great numbers. Encarnacion was named Blue Jays Player of the Year for 2012 as well as Most Improved Player.

* * * *

Edwin's nickname is E3. "Sometimes when my feet are slow, my throw [to first base] isn't good. But when I move my feet, the throw is straight every time," he explained. In May of the 2013 season, Encarnacion didn't exactly help his reputation for faulty fielding. Trying to make a catch of a pop-up, he tripped over the mound. After the game, Jose Bautista was one of several teammates all too willing to offer helpful advice: "I reminded him that there was a mound in the middle of the diamond."

* * * *

Players and fans notice everything and soon took note of Encarnacion's unique home run trot. After clubbing 42 homers in 2012, it was hard not to notice. Many of his long balls were tape-measure jobs and all eyes were on him as he rounded the bases. He has a tendency to keep his right arm motionless, as if it's in an invisible cast. One wag dubbed it "The Edwing." It can best be described as the way you might hold your arm while carrying an especially offensive bag of doggy-do.

* * * *

On April 30, 2013, E3 went where few men have ever gone without a ticket or a hotel key—into the fifth storey of Rogers Centre. This was a majestic upper, upper deck shot that filled the senses. In addition to the visual, it came with its own sound effects—first the distinctive sound of bat meeting ball, and then the audible gasps from the packed house, followed by applause. It was his first of two blasts and came off an all-star pitcher, Red Sox starter Jon Lester. It was measured at a modest 427 feet, but only the 500-level fence kept it from a much longer journey.

* * * *

His second signing with Toronto came in December 16, 2010, but the 2011 campaign started slowly for him. After struggling at the plate, it was felt that he might benefit from being relieved of third-base duties. The move to DH rejuvenated his bat, and he hit the 100th homer of his career, against the Minnesota Twins, and finished the season with 17 homers. He finished the year with a personal high of 34 doubles.

Playing at home against the visiting Seattle Mariners on September 13, 2012, Edwin hit his 40th season homer off talented pitcher Felix Hernandez. He also achieved the 100 RBI level. Both marks were personal highs. Encarnacion's offensive breakout was rewarded by the Baseball Writers' Association of America (BBWAA). He was named Toronto Blue Jay Player of the Year and received the Blue Jays Most Improved Player Award.

* * * *

Seven was indeed a lucky number for Edwin Encarnacion on Friday, July 26, 2013. The Blue Jays were playing the Houston Astros at the Rogers Centre and were looking to turn around what had so far been a miserable season with little for fans of the last-place Jays to applaud. It was the seventh inning and the Jays were down by a run, 6-4. Encarnacion was first up against Paul Clemens, and he hit a line shot homer to left that was moving with such speed it appeared to have a contrail. Later he said he was just trying to put the ball in play, adding, "I put it in play and I got a homer." E3's shot prompted the other Jays' bats to spring to life in a manner that would have made Mister Geppetto proud. Adam Lind followed with another long ball, this one landing in the right-field bleachers. Encarnacion then stepped to the plate again—this time against reliever Hector Ambriz—and his muscle memory must have been fresh because he struck an exact duplicate of the first shot, this drive barely clearing the left-field fence, and four Jays crossed the plate. The fans demanded a curtain call, and Edwin ducked briefly out of the dugout to oblige with a wave. They had entered the half-inning down by two and found themselves suddenly up by six. They held on to double the hapless Houstonians 12-6. It was E3's sixth grand slam. The cleanup hitter really cleaned up, going 3-for-4 with 5 RBI.

It was the second time that a Blue Jay player had homered twice in the same inning. The first was Joe Carter in that glorious summer of 1993. In Carter's October 3, 2-in-1 performance at Camden Yards in Baltimore, it was icing on the cake of what proved to be a championship season. In Encarnacion's case, it provided some much-needed nutrition for a win-starved, celebration-ravenous fan base. "To get to see something you only get to see once every 20 years is like seeing a comet," said starter R. A. Dickey after the game.

The offensive outburst by the Jays tied a team record for extra base hits, with 12. Jose Reyes and Brett Lawrie also contributed home runs for Toronto.

MARK EICHHORN

Mark Eichhorn was brought to the Blue Jays spring training camp in 1986 because they needed someone to throw batting practice. His throwing motion had been a work in progress, starting with a traditional over-the-top delivery and then morphing into a radical submarine approach. During spring training he decided to move his arm slot somewhere in between and repeated that motion until he was in a comfortable groove. The right-hander finished his delivery with a distinctive little chicken-hop sidestep. All of a sudden, Eichhorn had the rapt attention of the pitching coach and soon the Jays were shopping around for another batting practice pitcher. The new motion put a minimum amount of stress on his arm, allowing him to pitch more often. "The way I throw, I never get tired," he claimed. He promptly won 14 games and saved 10 on the strength of an impressive 1.72 ERA. He told *SI*, "I think a lot of people thought I might be a fluke because I was so different."

Eichhorn was a reliever for the Blue Jays in 1987, specifically a set-up man for closer Tom Henke. "The key is depth and contrast," said Eichhorn. "I come in there and throw my 72-mile-an-hour Frisbees so when Henke comes in, it looks like he's throwing 150 miles an hour."

EXHIBITION STADIUM

Stealing a nickname that Cleveland, Ohio, would gladly have given them for free, some writers referred to Canadian National Exhibition Stadium as "the mistake on the lake." These critics were in the minority, however. Fans came to love the old ballpark with all its shortcomings and eccentricities. It was the home park for the Jays for more than ten years and still holds many memories for longtime fans.

Then-rookie Paul Hodgson remembers his first introduction to the CNE field. "Bob Bailor took me out to the outfield and says, 'Hey kid let me show you something.' He put a ball down and it started rolling, and at a pretty good clip. Barry Bonnell came over and said, 'Look at this.' There were seams that were apart by about half an inch. Inside you could see what looked like carpenter's nails and the sharp ends were up, almost like they were hooked. Nail heads and the actual nail points where they were separated. That was nasty."

RON FAIRLY

The first player to represent both Canadian ML teams in the All-Star Game.

JOHN FARRELL

John Farrell was manager of the Toronto Blue Jays for only two years, 2011 and 2012, before moving on to lead the Boston Red Sox to the 2013 World Series championship.

"I think, if memory serves me correct, I was traded," said John Farrell in response to a question asked when the newly minted Red Sox manager met members of the Toronto press corps during a spring training game between his old and new teams. Technically he was correct. During the off-season before the start of the 2013 season, Blue Jays manager John Farrell was "traded" to the Boston Red Sox. In return for the skipper, the Blue Jays got pitcher Mike Aviles. But there is no doubt that he wanted out of Toronto and so the answer brought smiles to many faces.

When Farrell decided to abandon ship, the Jays were a very different group than the one that Farrell's Red Sox would battle for AL East supremacy. Names like R. A. Dickey, Jose Reyes, and Melky Cabrera had transformed them, on paper at least, into a manager's dream.

One thing was certain—Farrell's perceived lack of loyalty to the Blue Jays, a team that had given him a chance to manage in the big leagues, combined with the fact that he left town with several coaches, had only added fuel to the competitive fires that burn between these two AL East franchises.

Jays catcher J. P. Arencibia, who was given his first big break by Farrell, said, "He's the enemy when the game starts. He's a great person. But he's still the enemy." He added, "If that's his dream and where his heart is, then I'd rather him be in Boston than be here with his heart somewhere else."

John Gibbons, about to start his second stint as Jays manager, was asked his opinion. He wanted no part of the controversy. "Are we supposed to go out there and have a wrestling match or something?" he asked. "He's a little bigger than I am."

JUNIOR FELIX

His nickname was "Cat," and he entered the major leagues on May 4, 1989, by pouncing on the first big league pitch he ever saw and driving it over the fence for a home run. The blow came off Canadian Kirk McCaskill in a 3-2 extra-inning loss to the Angels at Exhibition Stadium. Brett Lawrie also homered in his first at-bat as a Jay, also on the first pitch, in 2011.

* * * *

Baltimore Orioles scout Ed Farmer's assessment of Blue Jays rookie Junior Felix was short and to the point. "If he's Junior Felix, I'd really love to see Senior Felix," he said.

* * * *

All those clichés about no lead ever being safe at Fenway Park are true. On June 4, 1989, the Blue Jays learned the power of persistence and patience when playing at the storied ballpark. At the end of six innings, the Red Sox and starting pitcher Mike Smithson held a 10-0 lead over the visiting Jays. Smithson was forced to leave the game in the 7th inning due to a blister on his foot.

The Jays came storming back, scoring 2 runs in the 7th, 4 in the 8th, and 5 in the 9th. The Red Sox rallied to tie the game in the bottom of the ninth. Junior Felix capped the amazing Jays comeback in the top of the 11th with a 2-run home run. The final score was 13-11, and it marked the biggest blown lead in the Red Sox's long history.

* * * *

On June 2, 1989, Junior Felix became the only visiting player to hit an inside-the-park grand slam home run at Fenway Park. It came with two down in the top of the ninth inning off reliever Bob Stanley with Ernie Whitt, Rance Mulliniks, and Nelson Liriano aboard and helped lead the Jays to a 7-2 victory.

TONY FERNANDEZ

"The all times hit leader and someone I always respected because he played hurt and injuries never stopped his career," Jerry Howarth explained. "In fact he would work even harder in his re-habbing and you'd always seen him with certain exotic exercise gadgets and doing things with pulleys in the clubhouse. Naturally his nickname became Mr. Gadget. He always wanted to be in the lineup. Even when he played hurt he played well."

Fernandez came from the infielder incubator, the shortstop starting point, the fielding foster home, the groundball graveyard that is the Dominican Republic. Whatever honors he has received in baseball—and they are numerous and prestigious—none are as meaningful as being called one of the best shortstops to come from that island nation of middle infielders.

* * * *

Fernandez's nickname back in the Dominican was "Cabeza," or "Head." It was hung on him due to the size of his head, which in bobblehead fashion, seemed out of proportion to the rest of his skinny body. "Tony was a little child with a big head," his sister Gloria (he had four sisters and six brothers, one his twin) told *Sports Illustrated.* "He never said anything about the baseball, but he was always practicing it."

* * * *

Thanks to his range, Fernandez often led American League shortstops in total chances. This fact alone puts his accomplishments in a special category because the degree of difficulty in his throws to first was upped. He often leapt into the air to make the submarine throw that was his trademark. "He makes the spectacular commonplace," observed former teammate Garth Iorg. Writer Ivan Maisel suggested that Fernandez had "the range of a Texas cattleman." And he was very much at home on that range, playing the game with a grace and elegance worthy of the ballet.

* * * *

In 1979, Toronto signed Fernandez as a 17-year-old amateur free agent. He made his big-league debut in 1983 and then spent the first eight years of his career with the Jays. Fernandez picked up four consecutive American League Gold Glove Awards from 1986-89, establishing himself as one of the best defensive shortstops in the game.

In 1990, Toronto traded Fernandez and Fred McGriff to the Padres in exchange for Roberto Alomar and Joe Carter. Alomar and Carter went on to help the Blue Jays capture their first World Series title in 1992.

Fernandez wouldn't be left out two years in a row, though. After being dealt to the Mets prior to the 1993 season, Toronto reacquired the legendary shortstop in a trade the following June. Fernandez then led the Jays with a .333 batting average and nine RBI in the team's second-straight World Series victory.

* * * *

"Fernandez had a big smile for everyone and played the game with great passion," Jerry Howarth says. "The man could hit. He was a switch-hitter par excellence who helped the Blue Jays— with his bat and glove—win the 1993 World Series."

All together, Fernandez was a member of the Blue Jays for parts of 12 seasons, including his final year in 2001.

* * * *

The thing about Tony Fernandez was that he made it look so easy. Almost maddeningly easy to those of us who know how hard the game really is. The ability to go deep in the hole to reach ground balls he had no right to reach. The way he seemed to glide, rather than run. The accurate submarine-style throws to first after a diving stop. The often off-balance throws that were invariably executed to perfection. The rainbow throws that seemed timed to arrive a half-step before the hopeful runner in order to inflict maximum psychological damage and frustration. "Fans will always remember his fluid motion from the hole at short," Howarth recalls. "Retiring runners at first with those long, looping throws that seemingly took forever to get to the bag, but were always there just in time for the out."

* * * *

Then there was his knack of getting a hit at just the right time. Even the way his cap sat precariously on his head, never pulled down tightly like that of other ballplayers, and the bill always straight, the way it came from the box. From the time he arrived in Toronto in 1983 for a 15-game tease, everyone knew that he was something special. The next year—his official rookie campaign—he led the Jays to their first American League East title.

* * * *

Fernandez's batting stance was not a thing of beauty, but for fans it was a joy forever. It was roughly based on the stance of his hero, Hall of Famer Rod Carew. Tony's, however, might best be described as "the Bizarro Carew." Or "the maestro," since he wielded the Louisville Slugger more like a baton than a bat. Or perhaps it was more like Itzhak Perlman, because he looked like he was trying to perfect the use of the world's first two-handed violin bow. Like Carew, he gripped the bat softly and changed his stance according to the pitcher and the situation. It was a corkscrew affair that had him holding the bat as if it were an afterthought. But it was far from that. "You don't show any kind of fear," he once said of his approach to hitting. "The pitcher is trying to intimidate you. Maybe the catcher can see fear. How are you gripping the bat? How is the leg?"

* * * *

His reputation soon spread throughout baseball. He was named to three all-star teams in the next five years and earned four consecutive Gold Gloves.

When he finally hung them up, he was the franchise leader in hits (1,583), games played (1,450), and triples (72). He also ranked third in batting average (.297).

Despite all his accomplishments as a Blue Jay, he left Toronto with unfinished business pending. He had not won a World Series as a Jay. That just didn't seem fair. After winning the world championship in 1992, the Jays brought him back in June of 1993. The move wasn't based on sentiment alone—far from it. The now-veteran shortstop batted .306 in 94 games and sparked the Jays to a second consecutive Fall Classic appearance. Once there, he excelled, driving in nine runs in the six-game series and batting at a .333 clip.

Tony Fernandez is on almost everyone's short list of the greatest Blue Jays ever. He played so beautifully at shortstop that he was sometimes called the American League's answer to Ozzie Smith.

MIKE FLANAGAN

When Flanagan arrived during the 1987 stretch drive, he made an immediate difference. In one game he was cruising along with a 6-1 lead in the seventh inning. At that point, Ernie Whitt was brought in to catch. The first pitch that Whitt called for was struck for a home run. So was the second. At this point Whitt made a trip to the mound. Flanagan looked at the catcher blankly and said "Are you on my team?"

His sense of humor did not go unrecognized, either.

"[Mike] was someone who always had fun, always ready with a quick quip. He could really turn a phrase," Jerry Howarth said. "He was serious at the same time and contributed to a lot of great teams. What I'll always remember about Mike is his great sense of humor and how much fun everybody had around him, myself included. We would go back and forth and tease one another and yet when push came to shove the professionalism came out and that's what you want. It's one thing to be cute and funny and have good stories, but you have to be able to perform at the major league level and Mike was able to do both."

* * * *

When Nolan Ryan struck out 14 Blue Jays in six innings in a 1989 matchup, and still lost the game 4-0, Flanagan suggested, "It looks like our problem this year has been not striking out enough." Flanagan went on to say that Ryan's success was largely due to the loud grunts he makes when he unleashes his fastballs. "I used to throw much harder myself," he said, "but I tore my vocal cords when I was a kid and haven't thrown as hard since."

* * * *

When the Blue Jays traded teammate Jeff Musselman to the New York Mets for a "player to be named later," Flanagan asked, reasonably, "Where are they going to find a player without a name? Are they going to find a ten-minute old baby whose parents haven't decided on a name? And let's be honest, how much could a player like that really help us?"

* * * *

When the Toronto Blue Jays proudly unveiled the new $500 million SkyDome in June of 1989, the stadium's most impressive feature was the retractable roof that could open or close within twenty minutes. The city and all of Canada were suitably impressed, as were Blue Jays players. All except for pitcher Mike Flanagan, that is. "It's great," he admitted, "but I was kind of hoping they'd have retractable fences."

* * * *

Flanagan wasn't a fan of the Big Apple. He once said: "I could never play in New York. The first time I ever came into a game there, I got into the bullpen car and they told me to lock the doors."

* * * *

When Flanagan was still pitching for the Baltimore Orioles, he was involved in a game in which the Blue Jays clubbed a record-setting 10 homers. A student of baseball history, he was asked about the offensive outburst after the game. "We tried looking for the record-breaking ball out beyond the fence in right, but there were too many of them all bunched up there."

* * * *

Blue Jays statistics may have to be adjusted downward, at least according to a theory once presented by Mike Flanagan, then with Baltimore. When fellow Oriole pitcher Mike Boddicker was clocked at an uncharacteristically high 88 mph in a game against the Jays in Toronto, Flanagan credited the added giddy-up to the exchange rate at the time. "We forgot to factor in the Canadian exchange rate," he pointed out. "It was really only 82 mph." Now, of course, with a stronger Canadian dollar, it would have been well over 90.

JASON FRASOR

Global warming and Jason Frasor have something in common. Despite vocal doubters and deniers, there is no doubt that they both exist, and they move with approximately the same speed. That is to say, glacial. Like watching paint dry, or hub caps rust, or the Senate debate a bill. The TV viewer sometimes is left to wonder if the delay was because he was unsure of what pitch to throw or whether to throw at all. Dictatorships were overthrown between the time he got the ball back from the catcher and the next pitch. The 5'9" right-hander was known as the "Sausage King," and surely it must be because his performances were long and drawn out and often hard to swallow.

Sometimes, one's eyes do deceive one, so it was nice to see this opinion confirmed by cold, hard facts. In 2012, *FanGraphs*, a site for stats nerds, ran the numbers on 426 pitchers (minimum of 30 innings pitched). Frasor was in eighth place in terms of his between-pitch pace. He also made the dubious top 35 in the previous three seasons.

* * * *

During his stay in Toronto, Jason Frasor took the mound in more games than any other Blue Jay pitcher in franchise history, a grand total of 505 appearances. That fact, combined with the fact that he was notoriously, shall we say, deliberate on the mound, might give some casual fans the impression that the reliever was the Jays' only pitcher during that period. His face seemed to be on TV as often as Peter Mansbridge or Ben Mulroney. Frasor was slow, so slow that hitters had time to not only ask the umpire about the previous pitch, but also find out about his wife and kids, where he grew up, what his hobbies are, his favorite foods, and his general philosophy of life. By the time his at-bat was complete, he knew enough to author the guy's biography.

Frasor came to the Jays in 2004 from the Dodger organization in exchange for Jason Werth. In a March 30, 2012, online article by Mike Rutsey for *Slam Sports*, he revealed how he got word of the trade.

"I remember walking into the [Dodgers] clubhouse and one of my teammates, I can't remember his name now, he said: 'Frasor, you're still here?' He knew before I did. I said: 'What do you mean?' Then I saw a coach and he walked me into the manager's office.

"But I'll never forget the 'Frasor, you're still here?'"

He went on to say, "Looking back it's the greatest thing that ever happened to Jason Frasor besides meeting my wife."

The Jays acquired Frasor, in hopes that he would be the answer to their closer problem and, splitting the role with Justin Speier, he validated GM Ricciardi's confidence in him, saving 17 games out of 19 tries. The following year, however, he was demoted to set-up man with Miguel Batista taking over the glory job. In 67 appearances, Frasor excelled, posting an ERA of 3.25. When B. J. Ryan became the closer (and briefly Jeremy Accardo), Frasor continued to perform well.

When Ryan went downhill in 2009, the Jays' brain trust again decided to split the closer duties, this time between Frasor and Scott Downs. He saved 11 games and turned in a fine 2.50 ERA. It looked like 2010 would be his breakout year as a closer, but following a disastrous start he again lost the coveted closer role and resumed his set-up role, where he registered 14 holds. His career trajectory seemed to literally be in a holding pattern.

DAMASO GARCIA

"Damaso Garcia was a very solid part of the '85 season and the 99 wins and the division championship," Jerry Howarth said. "He was a leadoff hitter and at that point statistics, Sabermetrics, and Moneyball were not part of the game, so while the numbers may not have added up there, Damaso was a key part of that team, leading off and playing second base. He was a very strong competitor but a good friend for a lot of players on that team. That's what you have to have for a team to bond."

During the 1986 season, Jays second baseman Damaso Garcia was a fixture in the Blue Jays doghouse and it looked as if he would be dealt to another team. The situation came to a head on May 14, as the Jays registered a tough 9-4 loss to the Athletics in Oakland.

After the game, Garcia was singled out for criticism by manager Jimy Williams. Williams suggested that Garcia's seventh-inning error had led to the loss, distracting starting pitcher Dave Stieb, who then served up home runs to Jose Canseco, Dave Kingman, and Mike Davis. The charge upset Garcia so much that he retreated to the clubhouse bathroom, removed his uniform jersey, hat, and sweatshirt, doused them with alcohol, and burned them.

Adding fuel to the fire, so to speak, was the fact that the Toronto Blue Jays and the Ontario Association of Fire Chiefs had just issued a Damaso Garcia baseball card with a fire tip on the reverse side. It read as follows: "Keep your infield free of errors. Remove all rubbish from your basement and attic."

Some people burn bridges; others burn laundry. He was quickly dealt to another team in a kind of fire sale.

CITO GASTON

Gaston took over as "interim" manager in May of 1989 when embattled skipper Jimy Williams was unable to lift the talent-laden team from last place. The former hitting instructor was initially reluctant, believing that he was "too friendly with the players." His pupils included Cecil Fielder and Fred McGriff. Once there, he became a lightning rod for criticism from fans. Some of the criticism may have been justified; most was not. Sure he could be unconventional, and some of his moves or non-moves left baseball traditionalists shaking their heads. Nevertheless, after two weeks, the "interim" label was removed and Cito became the manager. "After two weeks of doing it," he said cautiously, "it's not as bad as I thought. Not yet anyway." It would get worse before it got better, but in three years, he was destined to become the first black manager to win a World Series.

* * * *

Gaston was a second-guesser's dream. He did not manage by the book, and even when he did, he was usually on a different page

Photographed by Mike F. Campbell / 76wins

from his critics. Everyone in Toronto had an opinion about the enigmatic Texan. When the situation called for a steal, the runner often stayed put. If a pitcher looked ready for the showers, he was surprisingly allowed a chance to work his way out of trouble.

When a slow-footed player made it to first in a close late-inning situation, Cito did not send out a pinch runner. He even managed to cross up experienced announcers and former players like Tim McCarver during the '93 World Series. Sometimes, the moves or non-moves backfired and Gaston had egg all over his face; other times, the move caught the opposition off-guard and flat-footed. The fact that the manager had a talented team was both a blessing and a curse. When the Jays won, it was in spite of Cito. When they lost, he was invariably the goat. But if you thought that Gaston was managing by the seat of his pants, or worse—not managing at all, you'd be wrong. He was trying to "see into a game," get the feel for the game, and discover what might happen a few moves ahead. Perhaps that slow-footed runner might be needed for his bat in extra innings; maybe the pitcher had a proven advantage over the next few batters. No, he didn't manage by the seat of his pants but by his knowledge of the game and of his ballplayers. He managed more by intangibles than by the book.

* * * *

Perhaps the thing that most infuriated Cito's critics was his demeanor on the bench. He was just too placid, too unconcerned. He sat unmoved and unmoving, chewing his gum with gusto regardless of the situation playing out before him. Perhaps Canadians are used to hockey coaches, animated and shouting encouragement or disparagement. That's not baseball, and that's certainly not Cito Gaston. He had confidence in his players to do their job and his players worked hard to maintain that trust. His confidence instilled confidence.

JOHN GIBBONS

John Gibbons's ascension to major league manager was meritorious rather than meteoric. Once a humble bullpen catcher, the baseball version of stable boy, he still had the catcher's unblinking eye for all facets of the game. He is often criticized for being too country boyish, too lacking in charisma. The flip side of that is that he is by no means dismissive. He is genuine and unaffected in a job where cynicism and flippancy are endemic. That makes him an easy target for the media and, through them, the fans.

"For some reason, I'm viewed as a hick, a hillbilly, whatever that is," Gibbons has admitted. "That's not who I am. But because I talk a little different or walk a little different, that's life. I was born that way."

John Gibbons has a well-deserved reputation for being a straight shooter, a no-nonsense, old-school manager who expects his players to respect the team and the game. He began his first tenure as Blue Jays manager when Jay Ricciardi hired him to replace Carlos Tosca in the midst of the 2004 season. He was given a one-year contract for 2005, and this contract was quickly extended for three years.

* * * *

His reputation for being a player's manager is reinforced, rather than damaged, by four well-publicized spats with his own players. Their names are Hillenbrand, Lilly, Thomas, and most recently Brett Lawrie.

On August 21, 2006, the Blue Jays were at home to the first-place Oakland A's with Ted Lilly on the mound for the Jays. Lilly was in trouble immediately, allowing a pair of singles; however, he escaped the first inning without giving up a run. He recovered to pitch a hitless second. And then the roof fell in. In the third, he walked the first batter he faced and then was treated like a batting practice pitcher, with five straight Oakland hits. Manager Gibbons had seen enough and walked slowly to the mound to remove his pitcher. Lilly, no shrinking violet at the best of times, objected. The two had a heated back-and-forth before the pitcher finally handed the ball to Gibbons and left the mound. His final line was 7 earned runs and 8 hits in 2.1 innings of work.

Any pitcher worth his weight is reluctant to admit defeat and most managers are willing to ignore a small flare-up, but what happened next was less forgivable. Gibbons reportedly followed Lilly toward the tunnel from the Jays dugout and their dialogue continued to escalate. "Gibbons just went at him," said Canadian Press photographer Aaron Harris. "It looked like Gibbons grabbed him and they disappeared. Then the whole dugout emptied back there. It was mayhem down in the tunnel." Soon players ended the skirmish between the two and restored order if not peace.

Punches were allegedly thrown, although this was denied by both parties involved. Gibbons may or may not have sustained a bloody nose. "There were no punches thrown," said Lilly later, "so I don't think John had a bloody nose. I don't know how that would have happened." Gibbons tried to put it all behind them. "We've hashed all that out," he told *Fan 590*. "He thought he should have been left in the game," Gibbons said of Lilly. "I didn't think so." The next season, Lilly was pitching for the Chicago Cubs.

The second confrontation of note was with Shea Hillenbrand. Gibbons was reportedly incensed at comments Hillenbrand had written on the clubhouse bulletin board saying that the "ship was sinking." Hillenbrand did not accept the challenge and was soon dispatched to San Francisco. The incident died out, but bad feelings remained.

* * * *

At the beginning of the 2008 season, the Blue Jays were struggling to play .500 ball, and most observers were predicting Gibbons's departure as Blue Jays manager. Those predictions would later prove accurate. When they dipped five games below the .500 mark, he was cut loose on June 20th, only to return to the squad in 2013.

Prior to this, in the midst of the losing streak, the Jays were in New York to play the mighty Yankees. Reporters were gathered in the visiting manager's office at Yankee Stadium for the customary press scrum and the usual game-related questions were asked and answered. The conversation then turned to a *New York Times* story about a mathematician who had developed a system to rate the performance of Major League Baseball's 26 managers. "How'd I do?" inquired the embattled skipper.

"You were sixth," said a reporter.

Gibbons smiled broadly. Before he could comment further, another reporter added, "In the American League East."

What followed was a pregnant pause as everyone looked for the manager's reaction. The smile disappeared as Gibbons's eyes sought out and finally found the source of the comment. At that point the tough man's face dissolved into a smile, which quickly turned into a belly laugh that shook his entire body.

In actual fact, the mathematician had ranked Gibbons sixth-best *in all of baseball*.

* * * *

With a high-priced lineup estimated to be more than $125 million (US), it's fair to say that expectations were sky-high before the 2013 season. Before the first pitch was even thrown on Opening Day, a reporter asked John Gibbons if the news conference format would "be the same in the postseason." Now that's pressure. Those are expectations greater than even Charles Dickens's Pip had to deal with in *Great Expectations*, especially from a club that had gone 73-89 for a fourth-place finish the previous season."Let's hope so," Gibbons replied sheepishly.

* * * *

During his long baseball career, John Gibbons has seen his share of errors. He knows from experience that they can either be demoralizing, or they can be a building block to improvement. When Jeff Fuller bungled both the Canadian and American national anthems before a 2013 Jays spring training game he was disconsolate. As he was beating a hasty retreat, he ran into Gibbons, who greeted him with an outstretched hand and a few words of encouragement.

"Poor guy (had) nowhere to hide," recalled Gibbons. "I admire him for sticking it out there and doing it." The response to the incident said a lot about the character of the second-time-around Jays manager.

PAT GILLICK

Pat Gillick is in the Baseball Hall of Fame because of his pitching. Not the kind from the mound, although he did spend five years as a southpaw pitcher in the minor leagues. Gillick made the Hall because of his uncanny ability to make effective pitches to opposing teams and come away with franchise players. After a short stint in the minor leagues, Gillick turned to the front office. He won World Series titles with Toronto in 1992 and 1993 and added another in 2008 with the Philadelphia Phillies.

In twenty of his twenty-seven seasons as general manager, his teams won more than they lost, and he guided 11 teams to the playoffs.

Appropriately, he was inducted into the Hall of Fame in the same 2011 class as Roberto Alomar. It was his 1990 deal that sent Tony Fernandez and Fred McGriff to the San Diego Padres for Joe Carter and Alomar. Those two players led the team to back-to-back World Series championships and confirmed Gillick's reputation as a baseball genius/horse trader.

At the age of 26, Pat Gillick had a choice to make, as he was on the verge of going to law school and following a career in law enforcement. The romantic image of the FBI beckoned. Yet as luck would have it, in 1963, the former minor league southpaw was invited to become farm director in Houston. J. Edgar Hoover's loss eventually became the Jays' gain. After serving as coordinator of player development for the New York Yankees organization, in 1976, Gillick became an integral part of the Blue Jays expansion team. He began as VP of player personnel and eventually became VP of baseball operations.

* * * *

Former Blue Jays executive Pat Gillick felt that Rico Carty's demand for a three-year contract was a deal-breaker. It was 1979, and Carty was 39 at the time. "I don't mind paying a player," quipped Gillick, "but I don't want to pay for his funeral."

* * * *

Gillick's IQ is in the genius range and when he was pitching in the Baltimore Orioles farm system, he frequently amazed his teammates with his knowledge of baseball trivia. His uncanny ability earned him the nickname "Wolley Segap," which is Yellow Pages spelled backward.

TROY GLAUS

After playing his first six years as a member of the Anaheim Angels, Troy Glaus was sent to Arizona for the 2005 season. Despite back problems that hobbled him at third base, he socked 37 homers for the Diamondbacks, driving in 97 runs. Back in Toronto, the Blue Jays were in desperate need of a power hitter to replace the departed Carlos Delgado. The two teams forged a deal that sent Glaus and minor leaguer Sergio Santos to the Jays in exchange for Miguel Batista and Orlando Hudson.

"What you see is what you get and you always knew what you were going to get out of Troy," former teammate Matt Stairs said. "He was a solid third baseman, a solid hitter—the kind of player who could change a game with one swing, which is nice to have in the lineup."

* * * *

ALEX GONZALEZ

Alex Gonzalez was a good-looking hitter. Just ask any of the women who showed up to watch him play in Toronto. And apparently there were many. The interesting demographic factoid was confirmed in the fall of 2012 at an exhibition called "Baseball Hotties: Studs We Love" at the Louisville Slugger Museum and Factory in Kentucky. The retired Gonzalez was featured as one of the aforementioned studs. The exhibit also included Derek Jeter and Alex Rodriguez.

There is also a move afoot for fans to cast their votes on who should complete the inaugural lineup of "Baseball Hotties Hall of Fame." If selected, Gonzalez could be enshrined alongside the likes of heavy hitters Ted Williams, Jackie Robinson, and Roberto Clemente.

SHAWN GREEN

Shawn Green was one of the great Jewish ballplayers, a short but impressive list that also includes Hank Greenberg, Sandy Koufax, Rod Carew, and Moe Berg (the catcher and sometime spy of whom it was said "he could speak a dozen languages and couldn't hit in any of them"). The stereotype, of course, is that Jews are scholars, not athletes. These players and countless others dispel that myth.

Not that Shawn's family didn't place a premium on education, but in 1985, when young Shawn was batting a blistering .717 in Little League, the *Orange County Register*, his hometown California newspaper, ran a small story. It included the following classic line from his mother Judy, "If Shawn doesn't make the majors, he'll just become a doctor."

* * * *

Prior to one of the most emotionally charged All-Star Games in history in 1999 at Fenway Park, an ailing Ted Williams was brought onto the field in a wheelchair where he was mobbed by current stars, as if he were a rock star. After he had left the field and was being wheeled down the runway that leads to the clubhouse, Green sought and received an impromptu audience with the great man. They talked hitting for a solid five minutes. Later Green called it "one of the greatest thrills" of his life.

* * * *

Green played his first Major League game for the Blue Jays on September 28, 1993, and appeared in only two more games that season. Despite the fact that he did not take the field in the 1993 World Series, the team voted the future star a World Series ring. He was the second-youngest player in the Majors at the time. Not a bad way to start a career.

* * * *

In 1999, en route to a career-high 42 home runs, Green ventured into territory previously explored only by the likes of strongmen Jose Canseco, Joe Carter, and Mark McGwire. On April 22 the slightly built slugger pole-axed a pitch 449 feet. The ball landed in the fifth deck of SkyDome.

* * * *

The 1999 season turned out to be Green's last as a member of the Toronto Blue Jays. After the campaign, he was sent to the LA Dodgers along with teammate Jorge Nunez in a deal that brought Pedro Borbon Jr. and Raul Mondesi to Toronto. Green went out with a bang. Actually 42 bangs. He earned a first-class ticket to the All-Star Game with 25 first-half round-trippers and 70 RBI, a pretty good full season for most players. At the end of the season he had added another 17 homers (one every 14.6 at-bats) and had driven in a total of 123 runs while batting a career-high .309. His slugging percentage was .588. He topped the AL in doubles (45) and total bases (361). He left for LA with a Silver Slugger Award and a Gold Glove.

ALFREDO GRIFFIN

In 1979, Alfredo Griffin represented one of the first signs of spring in the seemingly endless winter of Blue Jays expansion. Mastermind Pat Gillick plucked him, along with Phil Lansford, from the Cleveland Indians in exchange for pitcher Victor Cruz.

Griffin made an immediate impact at shortstop, capturing AL Rookie-of-the-Year honors in 1979 (in a Major League first, Griffin actually tied for the honor with Minnesota Twins third baseman John Castino). In that freshman campaign, the instant fan favorite batted .287 with 179 hits and 10 triples. He also stole 21 bases. The Jays couldn't have asked for a better player or role model. He was at the leading edge of an influx of talented Dominican Republic players to the shores of Lake Ontario.

"Alfredo was a big part of the success story of the Blue Jays," Jerry Howarth said. "He's the answer to a great trivia question—who was on deck when Joe (Carter) hit that HR in '93? Yup, it was Alfredo Griffin and he was probably as happy as anybody that Joe cleared the deck right then and there and won that World Series."

* * *

Griffin's first stay in Toronto was from 1979 to 1984, when he was replaced by budding superstar Tony Fernandez. But after stints in Oakland with the A's and LA with the Dodgers, he returned just in time to win a World Championship with the 1992 Jays. It would be nice to say that he played an important role in that famous event, but that would be stretching the truth to the breaking point. Griffin was the prototypical good-field, no-hit shortstop but when he did manage to reach base, he was often a rally-killer. His steal percentage over 18 seasons was only 59 percent. In 1980 he managed 18 steals but was thrown out an astounding 23 times.

* * * *

When the Jays brought him back for the 1992 season, Griffin appeared in just 63 games and managed a .233/.273/.280 line with 10 RBI. In 1993, the final season of his career, Griffin appeared in just 46 games and managed a career-low .211/.235/.242 slash line with 3 RBI, 3 walks, and 3 doubles.

Currently a first base coach for the Los Angeles Angels, Griffin will be remembered by Jays fans for his glove, personality, and determination. He ranks 1st on the Blue Jays all-time list in sacrifice hits (74), 3rd in triples (50), 4th in caught stealing (74), and 8th in singles.

KELLY GRUBER

Toronto fans loved him, at least at first.

"He may be the most talented athlete the Blue Jays have ever had. He was an impact player and just a key part overall to that '92 team. At that point he was able to get a lot out of his ability," Jerry Howarth said.

The women also particularly adored him, and he was voted Toronto's most eligible bachelor.

Initially, he was Hollywood all the way. Later, when he was often on the bench with one injury or another, some fans liked to heckle him with shouts of: "Another hangnail injury, Kelly?"

* * * *

In 1990 Gruber struck for 31 homers and 118 RBI and was widely considered to be the best third baseman in the American League if not in all of baseball. And then his star began its descent. The next two years were, to be kind, sub-par. Boos replaced cheers and many of the jeers were vicious, inflicting pain. Injuries were a factor, but they didn't seem to be in proportion to his poor performance. He soon got the reputation as a malingerer. Even teammates and coaches were critical. Manager Cito Gaston could not disguise his frustration, telling reporters "I'm not talking about that—guy anymore. Go ask the trainers." He later added, in somewhat less inflammatory language,

"He's not one who can play through injuries." He paused before adding, "And he's been hurt all year."

Gruber's own words did little to rally support for the embattled player. In a city where hockey fans are used to seeing players shake off much more serious injuries, his comments brought further scorn.

"You either fold up or play, and I want to play," he once said. "If I feel good one day and terrible three days, at least I had that one day."

Nevertheless, he bristled at suggestions that he wasn't willing to sacrifice his body for the team. "No one knows how I feel but me. I just think if you have something to say, be man enough to say it to my face."

* * * *

It got so bad that even teammate Dave Winfield was taking shots. When second baseman Jeff Kent began filling in for Gruber at third, Winfield told Boston reporters, "Jeff Kent's been playing well, I mean really well. You've heard of that Wally Pipp story? It might be happening again." The fact that the comments were shown on the center field video screen at Fenway before a game between the Sox and Jays wasn't exactly a confidence boost for the embattled star.

Wally Pipp was the regular first baseman for the New York Yankees in 1925 when he developed a headache and was removed in favor of a kid named Lou Gehrig. Gehrig went on to play a record 2130 consecutive games, and Pipp went on to obscurity.

* * * *

How great a natural athlete was Gruber? In the early 1990s, a TV show called *The Superstars* featured athletes from various pro sports competing with each other. It was the ultimate "made for TV" sports event, but the competition was real— and it was intense. In 1991, Gruber was one of the contestants.

His competition included football players Jerry Rice, Herschel Walker, and Barry Sanders, fellow ballplayers Barry Bonds and Tim Wallach, and hurdler Renaldo Nehemiah, to name just a few.

When the dust had settled, Kelly Gruber was the winner, the first baseball player to lead the rest of the field. The final round pitted him against a field of much larger athletes, including Walker and Sanders. He won the swimming event easily, beating out runner-up Nehemiah by four seconds. Gruber wisely passed on the weightlifting event, won by Neal Anderson with a 320-pound effort.

Gruber not only won the kayaking race, but also he set a course record. He finished an impressive second in the basketball showdown and also in the cycling event. He then skipped the 100-yard dash to concentrate on the obstacle course. It was a wise move, as he hung on to win the overall competition with 31 points, 2 ahead of 2nd-place finisher Herschel Walker.

Kelly opted out of the 100-yard dash and before beginning the obstacle course. Despite the fact that Gruber didn't take 1st in that event, he had enough points to win the overall competition.

JUAN GUZMAN

Juan Guzman was a pitcher's pitcher. Jays reliever Duane Ward once observed, "He's got good stuff. When he doesn't have his good stuff, he still has good stuff."

* * * *

Originally signed by the LA Dodgers as an amateur free agent in 1985, Guzman arrived in Toronto in 1991, lost his first two starts, and then proceeded to win 10 straight games, finishing with a 10-3 rookie record. His fastball, consistently in the

95-mph range, can be described as recreational—it sometimes sank and sometimes sailed, leaving hitters to sink or swim. The native of the Dominican Republic also threw a wicked slider that acted like a split-finger fastball. In fact, he still takes pains to tell fans that are waxing nostalgic about his killer splitter, that it was actually a killer slider.

* * * *

The Jays got Guzman from the Los Angeles Dodgers in a September 22, 1987, trade for Mike Sharperson. Ironically, the Blue Jays wanted Jose Offerman, but Dodgers executive vice president Fred Claire was adamant that they take Guzman instead. "We wanted Offerman and thought we had the choice," Pat Gillick recalled. "In the end, Fred insisted it was his choice and gave us Guzman."

Gillick thought he'd been had. "I wasn't happy. Guzman had a good arm. We knew that, but a lot of young pitchers have good arms without ever putting it together."

Even after he became a Jay, Guzman initially got no respect. The Blue Jays did not protect him in the Rule 5 draft after the trade, meaning that any Major League team could have selected him for $50,000. Luckily, no team showed interest.

"How smart are we?" Gillick later asked no one in particular. Meaning, not very.

As for Claire, he was philosophical about the loss of a future all-star pitcher.

"The fact that 25 teams passed on him only last December is a reflection of the scouting reports," he said. "The fact that he wasn't protected is a reflection of what the Blue Jays thought about him, and they knew him better than anyone.

He added, "Sometimes you've got to be lucky—or maybe unlucky, depending on how you look at it."

* * * *

At first it looked like the Dodgers had indeed gotten the better of the Jays in the transaction. Guzman's minor league development with the Jays was slow and painful to watch. He pitched 310 innings from 1988-90, issued 231 bases on balls, and threw an alarming 40 wild pitches.

"He always threw 90-plus, but he just didn't have the poise and the command," said Guzman's 1990 manager, John Stearns, in 1992. "He used to stand on the mound and hold the ball. He would think too much." Jays roving pitching instructor Mel Queen identified the problem as being technical in nature, a simple matter of body mechanics and release point.

In the Jays' minor league system, Guzman was so wild that multiple baseballs were needed for his bullpen sessions.

"He'd throw 'em over the screen, the fence, whatever," former Toronto pitching coach Galen Cisco once said. Cisco had also been his mentor at Syracuse in Triple A in 1989. "You had to take five or six baseballs with you to the bullpen to get him loose before a game," he added.

In the majors, he continued to struggle with control issues, topping the AL in wild pitches in both 1993 and 1994. The upside was that with his fastball, few hitters were willing to dig in against him. It was Cisco who helped him to find a consistent release point.

* * * *

In 1996, Guzman boasted an ERA of 2.93, the stingiest in the junior circuit. His blazing fastball and effective slider confounded hitters throughout his career, helping him to run up a gaudy 7.5 strikeouts per nine innings lifetime.

* * * *

Guzman won 16 games in the Jays' historic 1992 season. His ERA was 2.64.

"The Blue Jays would never have won those two World Series in '92 and '93 without a complimentary starter and even though others got the praise, he was so solid in that third and fourth role as a starter. He not only gave innings to the staff but wins as well and he loved to compete. He just quietly went about his business and enjoyed everybody else," said Jerry Howarth.

* * * *

Jays teammate Paul Molitor once observed, "The only chance to beat him is when he beats himself." During the 1993 ALCS with the Chicago White Sox, Chisox outfielder Tim Raines suggested another method. "I was hoping someone might hit him with a line drive," he said.

* * * *

Guzman started his Toronto career with a bang. In his first three campaigns as a Blue Jay he had a combined 40-11 record and a 3.28 ERA—and was instrumental in leading the Jays to those consecutive World Series titles, although he didn't register a win in either October Classic. Nevertheless, his postseason record during that span was 5-1, and his ERA was 2.44.

* * * *

On the mound, Guzman was as methodical as Lee Strasberg and as deliberate as a Ron Maclean pun. At times it was hard to watch, as if he were debating with himself whether to throw the ball at all. Some Toronto fans took to calling him the "Human Rain Delay."

Roy Halladay

Keith Allison

Halladay actually has a save on his extensive pitching resume. It came in his official rookie year of 1999, as a member of the Blue Jays. The Jays had a sizable lead and brought Halladay in relief of starter David Wells. He pitched three innings in the eventual 9-3 Jays win. "I didn't realize that if you pitch three innings (to close the game) regardless of the score, it's a save," said Halladay. It's unlikely he will be called upon in such a role again any time soon. "It's kind of neat to have one," concedes the future Hall of Famer before adding, "I hope I never have a save opportunity again."

* * * *

Halladay, nicknamed "Doc," knocked on the no-hitter door in a 1998 game against the Detroit Tigers. In just his second major league game, 21-year-old Halladay tried to crash the exclusive no-hitter club on September 27, 1998. Unfortunately, with two outs in the ninth at SkyDome Bobby Higginson homered to delay his membership. Ironically, the homer was caught by Dave Stieb in the Toronto bullpen. At that time, Stieb was the only Blue Jay to have chucked a no-no.

* * * *

It was in 2002 that Halladay officially and emphatically laid claim to being the Jays' ace. He rang up a 19-7 record with a 2.93 ERA. Much of the previous two seasons had been spent in minor league outposts like Syracuse, Dunedin, and Tennessee.

Halladay had countless great moments as a member of the Blue Jays. One that stands out came on September 6, 2003, against the Detroit Tigers. On that day he pitched 10 innings of shutout ball en route to a Cy Young Award. Even though the '03 Tigers were relatively toothless, the very fact that Doc was still pitching in the 10th inning is incredible in this era of pitching specialization. The Tigers didn't register their first hit until the 8th inning, when pinch hitter Kevin Watt ruined the string with a one-out double. The entire game went only 2 hours and 3 minutes, a testament not only to his throwback-style endurance but to his economy of pitches. In fact his pitch total still came in under the 100 mark.

"The way Roy approached the game and the way he did his homework was impressive," Matt Stairs, once Halladay's teammate, said. "You knew he was there for one reason, and that was to pitch and win ballgames."

* * * *

On August 6, 2009, the highly satirical online "newspaper," *The Onion*, ran a story entitled: "Blue Jays GM Confirms There Never Really Was A 'Roy Halladay.'" Datelined Toronto, the article described a press conference in which Blue Jays general manager J. P. Ricciardi admitted there really was no such person.

Nevertheless, Ricciardi was trying to trade the non-existent rightie, and was demanding a fair price. "A 6-foot-6, 225-pound pitcher with a 94-mph fastball who plays 200 innings a season? We're not giving that guy away for just anything, even if he does not exist."

The Onion quoted Ricciardi complaining: "The best the Phillies could come up with was Kyle Drabek and a prospect to be fabricated later. You're going to have to do better than that if you want Roy Halladay."

The expose suggested that Halladay was actually an amalgam of statistics "compiled by Juan Guzman, Pat Hentgen, Woody Williams, Esteban Loaiza, Josh Towers, Gustavo Chacin," etc.

Ricciardi had supposedly given his creation his uncle's first name, and "whenever we needed a face, like for his baseball card, we just used a picture of our UPS guy."

Not willing to stop there, the parody said that there were many more fictitious Blue Jay stars, including Dave Stieb, Jesse Barfield, and Joe Carter. In a final display of sacrilege, they added that Carter's winning home run to capture the 1993 World Series was in reality "just a two-run single in the seventh inning by Paul Molitor."

When asked to explain his team's inactivity at the trade deadline, as the parody explained, Ricciardi bristled, saying, "Look, we are in fourth place in the toughest division in baseball, and the only way to remain competitive is by cutting salary, trading for prospects, and building for 2011."

"Obviously, if Roy Halladay existed, I would have traded him," he added. "I'm not an idiot."

* * * *

When Roy Halladay decided to hang up his cleats after the 2013 season, the two-time Cy Young winner looked north to Toronto. Plagued by back and arm injuries, the man who had retired so many hitters wanted to retire as a Toronto Blue Jay, the team that had given him his start in the game. The Jays organization was more than happy to oblige, signing him to a one-day contract so that he could end his brilliant career as a Jay. His career totals included a 203-105 record, a 3.38 ERA, 2117 strikeouts, 20 shutouts, and 67 complete games. He also tossed a perfect game in 2010 for his Philadelphia Phillies and followed up with a playoff no-hitter against the Cincinnati Reds in the postseason.

"He was the core of his team wherever he went—winning games and being a significant part of that team's success story," Jerry Howarth explained. "He was a leader in his own right, although probably for some teammates he seemed unapproachable because he was so intent on getting the most out of his day. Often teammates would be intimidated by him. I really had the ultimate respect for Roy."

JAY HAPP

Jay Happ is the only Peruvian to play for the Toronto Blue Jays. He hails from Peru, Illinois.

* * * *

Happ was the starter for Houston when Matt Cain spun his perfect game against the Astros on July 29, 2010.

* * * *

Happ came to the Jays in a July 20, 2012, multiplayer trade with the Houston Astros. He was a reliever until Brett Cecil faltered, at which point he took his place in the starting rotation. A fractured right foot cut his season short, but he was impressive enough to maintain his starting role at the beginning of 2013. He was sidelined by a hard-to-watch line drive to the head off the bat of Desmond Jennings in a game against the Tampa Rays on May 7, 2013. The sickening thud could be heard high above in the press box in Tampa. The crowd was struck silent as he lay on the mound for more than five minutes, being attended to by medical staff and strapped to an immobilizing backboard. When he was taken from the field on a stretcher, he still managed to acknowledge the encouraging applause from the crowd.

The injury reignited calls for better ways of protecting pitchers who are so vulnerable to such injuries. So far, there appears to be nothing on the sports equipment market that would protect the pitcher without compromising his ability to pitch.

* * * *

Until his injury, Happ had been one of the brighter lights to shine for the Jays in a disappointing start to what was expected to be a breakthrough season for the franchise. He had a 2-2 record with a 4.91 ERA and a WHIP of 1.55.

ROY HARTSFIELD

Being first isn't always easy—just ask Roy Hartsfield. Hartsfield was the original Blue Jays manager, holding the position for three years, from the unforgettable Opening Day of 1977 until his departure at the end of the 1979 season. In some ways you could compare that period to the first trimester of a very long gestation period for respectability.

Hartsfield was not hired for name recognition. Nor for charisma, although he possessed a surplus of southern charm. He had just three years of playing experience, and as a minor league coach, had flown beneath the radar of all but the most fanatic of baseball followers. He was hired because he had the qualities that were needed in guiding a young team—patience, understanding, and most importantly, an ability to teach. He would need iota of those qualities because his team consisted of players well past their sell-by date, players not yet ready for prime time, and a random assortment of position-fillers and cast-offs. He once admitted to a *Toronto Star* reporter, "The guys I managed the year before in Hawaii (in the triple-A Pacific Coast League) were probably a better team."

Among his more successful pupils were Ernie Whitt, Jim Clancy, and Dave Stieb, all of whom graduated with honors in the class of 1985 as division champions. Hartsfield was long gone by then, of course, but he had laid the groundwork and deserved some of the credit.

The Jays finished that first season with a record of 54 wins and 107 losses, 45 ½ games out of first in the seven-team AL East. Two more 100-loss seasons followed for Hartsfield, and it would be seven long years before the Blue Jays emerged, blinking and shading their eyes, from the American League East basement. When it finally happened, Hartsfield was long gone. But it's fair to say that he was the right man at the right time. As with Joey Smallwood when he guided Newfoundland into Confederation, he was a pioneer, breaking new ground and learning from mistakes. And make no mistake, there were lots of mistakes. But there were also encouraging signs. An amazing 77 of the 107 losses had been by one- or two-run margins. "If those 77 games had been decided by 10 or 12 runs, I'd feel a hell of a lot worse than I do now," Hartsfield said in a season postmortem.

Despite their last-place finish in 1977, there were moments that stood out for Hartsfield and his Blue Jays during that initial campaign. One of them was a late-season trouncing of the greatest franchise in baseball history, the New York Yankees. It happened at Yankee Stadium and was the worst beating the pinstripers had received in the 52-year history of the legendary ballpark. The final score was 19-3, with Roy Howell driving in an amazing 9 of those runs. In the clubhouse after the game,

Hartsfield was understandably wistful about the lopsided win. "I was thinking," he told reporters, "that maybe the league should allow expansion teams one concession—when we win like this, we should be allowed to put our excess runs into a reservoir and use them at a later date."

* * * *

Other highlights from that initial season came from opposing ball clubs. On June 8, Nolan Ryan struck out 19 Jays in a 2-1 win.

* * * *

In May of 1978, Hartsfield had this realistic but probably unnecessary message for Blue Jays fans. "Anyone who tells himself he can win a pennant with an expansion team is just spitting into a gale."

* * * *

In 1978, the Jays under Hartsfield "improved" to 59-103. They were still last, but on a brighter note, it was their best season ever. The highlight surely came on June 26 when they demolished the Baltimore Orioles 24-10. Unfortunately it was followed in 1979 by their worst record ever. In fact it was the worst record in more than six decades. The low light came in the form of a 24-2 embarrassment at the hands of the California Angels. (Said first baseman Craig Kusick, who was sent to the mound to mop up, "I just wanted to throw it down the middle so nobody got hurt.") Hartsfield was fired at season's end and never again managed in the majors. He was so hurt by the manner of his dismissal that he never returned to Toronto.

RICKEY HENDERSON

Jerry Howarth summarized the contributions of the greatest base stealer to play Major League Baseball: "Rickey just tormented pitchers, both patiently at the plate, and then especially on the bases. He's a Hall of Famer through and through and is a great addition to Cooperstown. He had fun with the fans in left field whether they were at home or on the road. I can't say enough about what he meant to that '93 team. He was just outstanding. We heard a lot about Rickey before he came to Toronto and then to see him play and to be with him was just a treat."

TOM HENKE

When your nickname is the Terminator, your career choices are limited. You can be a Mafia hit man, a pro wrestling villain, or a very successful relief pitcher. Tom Henke was the latter. The Terminator tag was originally bestowed by teammate John Cerutti after they went to see the Arnold Schwarzenegger movie of the same name in 1985.

Like Arnold, his catch phrase could have been "Hasta la vista, Baby!" because when he went to the mound, the game was pretty much over.

With his oversized, style-proof glasses and imposing 6'5", 225-pound frame, he resembled Clark Kent just before he stepped into the phone booth. Or perhaps a German U-boat commander. Once on the mound he became a super-reliever. Blessed with a blazing fastball and apparently in need of glasses, few batters were anxious to dig in against this guy. Complementing the heater with a very effective forkball, he struck out 9.8 batters per nine innings over this career.

* * * *

When Henke entered a game in Toronto, the ballpark was transformed into the House of Henkenstein. His fastball was nightmare-inducing and when he stuck in the forkball, it usually meant you were done. The term "relief pitcher" refers to the act of relieving a struggling pitcher, but it took on a whole new meaning when Henke walked to the mound. The feeling of relief that swept over the ballpark was palpable.

* * * *

In 1989, Tom Henke had the kind of year that most can only dream about. After a slow season start, he put the Jays on his back and took them all the way to the playoffs. From June 1 onward, he saved 18 games and posted a 1.02 ERA! That period included an incredible 19 mound appearances (27.1 innings) in which he allowed only one earned run. During the pennant stretch he became virtually unhittable. With the Jays neck and neck in September, he closed hitters down, winning two games, allowing less than a run a game (0.96), and striking out 25 in 18-and-a-third innings. He rang up three saves in all, including the one that took Toronto to the AL East title. Hitters managed just an anemic .205 batting average against him that year.

Tom Henke was one of the best closers in Blue Jays history. In his eight-year Toronto sojourn, from 1985-1992, the big right-hander recorded 217 saves while maintaining an ERA of 2.48. Henke had some monster years as a Jay moundsman, like 1987, when he recorded an American League-best 34 saves and a 2.49 ERA and earned all-star recognition. Other prime examples were in 1990 and '91, when he recorded back-to-back 32-save years. And then there was the 1992 world championship campaign. Henke rang up 34 saves with a microscopic 2.26 ERA in the regular season. But it didn't end there.

In the World Series against Atlanta under the pressure of the biggest in baseball, he added two more saves and a 2.70 ERA as the Jays brought the championship to Canada for the first time.

"When he was here from '85 to 1992 and winning that World Series in 1992, there was no one better as a teammate or as a closer," Jerry Howarth said. "Tom would get the job done when it counted and then celebrate with his teammates—because he knew he was one of 25, not just the one who stood out as the exemplary closer."

There was just one spectacular glitch on his World Series resume. In the ninth inning of Game Six, he blew the save. But all was forgiven when the Jays won the game in extra innings. After the World Series, the Blue Jays opted to give Duane Ward the role of closer, and Henke moved back to Texas where his career had begun.

* * * *

In 1991, Henke established a new Major League record for consecutive saves with 25. The record-setter came against the Detroit Tigers on August 7 in a game that Juan Guzman had started. Guzman had gone seven innings before being replaced by Duane Ward, who retired all three batters he faced in the eighth. The Terminator finished the Tigers off in the 9th, saving a 5-2 victory and breaking the record. The streak came to an end, thanks to future Blue Jays hero Paul Molitor. Playing for the Milwaukee Brewers, Molitor hit a 3-run homer off the big man to beat the Jays 5-4 on August 13, 1991. The streak had begun on April 9.

Henke was inducted into the Canadian Baseball Hall of Fame and Museum on June 18, 2011. In all, he pitched in 446 games wearing a Blue Jays uniform and finished his Major League career with 311 saves.

"I've always considered Toronto and Canada my favorite place to play and to help to bring home Canada's first World Series win can never be duplicated," he said on the eve of his induction. Overall, Henke appeared in five postseason series: 4 ALCS and one October Classic. His ERA was 1.83.

* * * *

Henke almost escaped. He almost made it through his entire baseball career without having to feel the same sense of failure he brought to countless hitters across baseball. In his final year before retiring, he was playing for the National League St. Louis Cardinals, who were then coached by Joe Torre. Torre was short of pinch hitters, so reluctantly he asked Henke to hit for himself in an 8th-inning situation that called for a pinch hitter. He gave his hitting virgin a stern warning: Do not try to get a hit. Just take three pitches and get ready to pitch the 9th inning. But Joe overlooked the competitive juices that flow in all of us—even pitchers—when facing a challenge. "I got a little stubborn out there," Henke told Jays radio announcers Alan Ashby and Jerry Howarth recently. He proceeded to foul off pitch after pitch in the chill weather.

When he was finally retired and took the mound, the cold had impacted his feel for the ball. He proceeded to walk the bases full before finally escaping harm. But he did not escape a tongue-lashing from Torre after the game.

"I understand what happened, Tom," said the manager. "But when I tell you to take three pitches, you take three pitches."

* * * *

Ted Williams used to enjoy watching Henke pitch on TV at his salmon fishing lodge in New Brunswick. "He's a good pitcher," said the mortal enemy of pitchers. "I like him. They swing at a lot of bad pitches on him. He must have a good slider."

Aaron Hill

"Aaron Hill was young when he first came up. He was a spark-plug, and a lot of things happened when he was on the field." – Jerry Howarth

* * * *

When the Kansas City Royals' Mike Sweeney successfully stole home against Yankee pitcher Andy Pettitte, Blue Jays coach Brian Butterfield took note. Sweeney had taken advantage of Pettitte's famous focus and turned that strength into a weakness.

When the Jays and Yankees next faced each other during the 2007 season, Butterfield put his players on high alert. If someone reached third base with two out, they should be prepared to steal. As *Sports Illustrated* later reported, Jays second baseman Aaron Hill received the instructions with trepidation.

"Hill doesn't have the personality of someone who would steal home on his own," *SI* suggested. "He's the paratrooper who doesn't so much jump out of the airplane as get pushed."

"You're hot." Third base coach Butterfield had approached base runner Hill from behind to speak these words to him in hushed tones. Lest you get the wrong idea, the message had nothing to do with Hill's youthful good looks, or even his current hitting status. The score was 1-1 in the seventh inning and the Jays had runners on first and third with two out against Yankees ace Andy Petttitte in this game at Rogers Centre. As fate would have it, Hill had ended up on third and now had run the count to one ball, no strikes.

Butterfield gave Hill his instructions. "If the count gets to 1 and 1, you're hot," he said. "I was almost thinking," recalled Hill *Oh, please, don't throw a strike*. I was starting to breathe heavy. Next pitch is strike one. So there I go."

Pettitte is notoriously stingy in giving up runs, and the Jays knew it. The coded message told Hill that he had the green light to steal home if the opportunity presented itself. The New York southpaw was on a short list of pitchers deemed vulnerable to the rare steal of home. Although he had one of the best pick-off moves to first in recent baseball history, he was also slow and methodical in his pre-pitch routine.

Pettitte was needlessly focused on the runner at first, lead-footed catcher Jason Phillips. Hill took a cautious lead and when he broke for the plate, it took a split second for Pettitte to realize what was happening and another split second to react. He looked like a deer frozen in the headlights. By the time he had thawed, it was too late. When he did throw to catcher Jorge Posada, it was a feeble attempt, chest-high, and Hill slid in well under the tag.

It's tough to draw up such a play because there are so many variables involved, but all the conditions were there—a perfect storm for stealing success.

The play came with two outs to break a 1-1 tie in Toronto's series-clinching 3-2 win.

"I definitely felt my heart beating, that's for sure," Hill said later. "I've never done that. I didn't know what was going to happen. I just pictured the umpire calling me safe and hoped that'd give me a little extra boost."

When they saw him break for the plate, Yankee infielders started yelling "Home! Home!" and as *SI* reported, "Hill remembers that as the sound track to the longest and fastest run of his life." But Hill was now committed and he slid in before the tag. "The adrenaline rush just took over," he said. "It was amazing. Probably one of the best moments of my career."

Pettitte, a pitching perfectionist, took full responsibility for success of the play. The Blue Jays ended up winning the tight contest 3-2 on an Adam Lind double, but the steal was the play everyone was talking about. Hill had stolen the show and the game.

It was the first straight swipe of home for the Jays since Raul Mondesi did it on April 17, 2001, against these same Yankees.

ERIC HINSKE

Eric Hinske was the 2002 AL Rookie of the Year for the Toronto Blue Jays. After leaving Toronto, he played in three consecutive World Series with the Red Sox in '07, the Tampa Bay Rays in '08, and the Yankees in '09. The '07 Red Sox and '09 Yankees teams captured world championships. Tampa Bay lost to the National League champion Philadelphia Phillies in five games.

* * * *

Toronto TV color man Pat Tabler summed up Eric Hinske's failure to swing at good pitches: "Paralyzation due to over-analyzation," he quipped.

* * * *

In a Red Sox–Jays game in 2006, Hinske was hit by a pitch from Red Sox reliever Keith Foulke. The two engaged in a dialogue as he made his way to first. After the game, Hinske revealed what had been said. "He said on the mound he didn't try to hit me. I just looked at him and said, 'Come on man.' It really hurt. He nearly took my nipple off."

* * * *

In December of 2013, Hinske was named as first base coach of the Chicago Cubs.

Paul Hodgson

He played only 20 games in the Major Leagues, in baseball terms little more than "a cup of coffee." Call it a cup of Tim Horton's since Paul Hodgson was a member of an exclusive fraternity of Canadians who have played for the Blue Jays. Hodgson learned the game in the baseball-rich province of New Brunswick, signing with the Jays as an amateur free agent on his 17th birthday.

Born in Montreal, the Marystown, NB, native made his big league debut in 1980 at the age of 20. At the end of the season he was returned to the minors and by the ripe old age of 23 his career was over.

As a Jay he batted a modest .220 and his first home run was also his last, but Blue Jays fans were pulling for the second Canuck (Dave McKay was the first) to play for the young franchise. Blessed with all the tools—superior bat speed, speed afoot, and a strong throwing arm—the lanky outfielder caught the attention of scouts Wayne Morgan and Bob Prentice. After a tryout for Pat Gillick, he was signed.

"My first at-bat was against Minnesota Twins starter Jerry Koosman," recalls Hodgson. "I remembered him well from the Miracle Mets of 1969. I had watched that World Series. This was my first start and first at-bat. Koosman had white hair by then and he must have been pushing 40, but he was still throwing 90-92 mph and mixing it with a nasty over-the-top curve ball that fell off the table. The first pitch he threw was a fastball, armpit high and a foot outside. The umpire was Kunkel and he says, 'Strike!' Twins catcher Butch Winegar actually laughs, and the ump winks and says, 'Welcome to the show kid.' It was right out of a bad movie. My first hit came off Doc Medich of the Texas Rangers a few days later."

* * * *

Life in the minors is full of pitfalls. The bus travel is brutal, the pay is low, and the fans can be unruly. Of course you can generally tolerate the boos, but when you start hearing a hissing sound, pay attention.

As Hodgson explained, "I was playing in Medicine Hat, Alberta, and us new guys were curious about the town. Over some beers, one guy gave us some strange advice. He said to make sure we walked away from the stands when we exited the locker room. He explained that the way the ballpark was configured, fans could drop something on top of your head as you came out. 'Walk along the fence,' he warned us. Naturally we asked why. He explained that a high-round draft pick had pitched there but the guy couldn't get anyone out. One night he was getting bombed and a fan dropped a rattlesnake on him from the top row. Who comes to the ball park with a rattler? Good question, but this guy was waiting for him to screw up and that's what happened. I paid attention to that! I don't think anyone hated our team members like they hated this guy."

ROY HOWELL

On September 10, 1977, Roy Howell led the Jays to a brutal 19-3 assault on New York Yankee pitchers. The Jays were almost 40 games behind the Yankees in the standings, but you wouldn't have guessed it from this wipeout. Howell drove in 9 runs on the strength of 5 hits, 2 of them homers, and 2 doubles. His first double came against New York starter Catfish Hunter. It was the biggest drubbing the Yankees had endured in fifty years, as the Jays pounded out 20 hits against five Yankee hurlers. The 19 runs scored and 20 hits were obviously franchise records. Jim Clancy recorded the win for Toronto.

The outburst was especially welcome since the Jays had managed to score only 14 runs in their previous nine games and had recorded a single win in the previous 14 games.

GARTH IORG

Garth Iorg was selected by the Jays in the 1976 expansion draft from the New York Yankees organization. Iorg was a lifer, playing only for the Jays during his nine-season big league career and retiring as the Jays' all-time pinch hitting leader.

Iorg's nickname was surely one of the best in baseball, if only because it makes so much sense and so little sense at the same time. His teammates called him "Monster" because his last name sounds like the noise a monster might make. You gotta love that.

* * * *

When Iorg came to the plate, Jays fans greeted him with chants of "Orgy! Orgy!" You've gotta love that, too.

* * * *

Iorg's batting stance has been described as "eccentric" and likened to a helicopter about to take flight. His weight was on his back foot and only the toes of his front foot made contact with the ground. His bat was poised horizontally over his head as if he was using an invisible level. He leaned back toward the catcher as if to get as far away from the pitcher as possible.

CLIFF JOHNSON

Cliff Johnson was a needler and some of his jibes were not appreciated by teammates. Among those who had a problem with him were George Bell and Damaso Garcia. Garcia called Johnson "Mule Face."

* * * *

In 1981, when he was a member of the Texas Rangers, an informal poll of players indicated that Johnson possessed the "biggest swing" in the American League.

* * * *

Johnson was a good-hit, no-field ballplayer. Legend has it that he once took his bat to church to be blessed. A teammate asked, "Did he bring his glove, too?"

JOSH JOHNSON

Josh Johnson was part of the 12-player swap that had the baseball world all a-Twitter before the start of the 2013 baseball season. In truth, he was the key guy for Blue Jays general manager Alex Anthopoulos. There's no doubt that it is a name to be reckoned with. The powerful right-hander had been a member of the Marlins organization since he was first drafted in 2002.

His fastball is overpowering and with a rebuilt curveball and proven slider in his utility belt, he has everything it takes to be an integral part of the Blue Jays' rotation. If not yet an ace, he's certainly a big card in the Jays deck. A shoulder injury in 2011 sidelined him and in 2012 he posted a less than impressive 8-14 record with an ERA of 3.81. But the Jays were thinking more about the healthy Johnson, the one who went 11-6 in 2010 and had a sterling 2.30 ERA with 186 strikeouts. There were signs of the old Josh at the tail end of 2012 and the Jays look to build on those positives and rebuild the shaken confidence of their new acquisition.

KELLY JOHNSON

Oops! When second baseman Kelly Johnson was traded from the Arizona Diamondbacks to the Blue Jays on August 23, 2011, in exchange for Aaron Hill and John McDonald, he was scheduled to play the next day at Rogers Centre. He was a no-show. Injury? No. Contractual squabble? Nope. Sporting a .209 batting average, the 29-year-old was already a borderline player—that border being the Mendoza Line—but he apparently knew little about the border between Canada and the United States. It seems that he arrived in Toronto without a passport and had to return to Arizona to retrieve it. He debuted on August 25 and went one-for-two with a couple of walks.

REED JOHNSON

Reed Johnson played for the Jays from 2003-2007. He is one of a handful of players who have hit a leadoff and walkoff homer in the same game. His came during the 2003 season. Adding to his leadoff credentials was a tendency to get hit by pitches with alarming regularity. On two separate occasions, he was struck by pitches three times in a game.

TIM JOHNSON

The Tim Johnson saga is both sad and shameful. He began his tenure with the Blue Jays with so much hope, but now will be remembered for one thing and one thing only—lying about his Vietnam combat record.

It's hard to go from being a Major League manager to virtual banishment from the game you love. And the game that once loved you. When he was a coach in Boston under Kevin Kennedy, the players had a fierce loyalty to him. The same thing happened when he took over the show in Toronto in 1998. He knew the game well enough to lead the Jays to 88 wins, the most since the glory days of 1992 and '93.

He was genuinely a great motivator and a great leader of men. Unfortunately the motivation and leadership were built on quicksand.

MUNENORI KAWASAKI

Munenori Kawasaki arrived suddenly, like a SSD (spontaneous synchronized dance).

Sometimes called Muni, Kawasaki is a living bobblehead, seemingly a mascot who can also play. He waves to the crowd, dances in the dugout, and fakes stealing bases in a hilarious pantomime of running.

The catchy ad for the motorcycle of the same name said "Kawasaki lets the good times roll." The same could be said of the ballplayer. Within five games—surrounded by a team of stars—it was Kawasaki's name that the fans at Rogers Centre were chanting. With his baseball actions interspersed with bows, smiles, impromptu headstands, and dugout dancing that defies description, the baby-faced, impish, ever-grinning ballplayer was an instant fan favorite.

* * * *

Even before he came to the Blue Jays, Kawasaki got Adam Lind's attention. He recalls a 2012 game when the Jays were playing Kawasaki's Seattle Mariners. Kawasaki worked a walk and then greeted first baseman Lind with an enthusiastic "Konichiwa!" That's when Lind knew that this guy was not your usual shy, close-mouthed rookie. In the next game in the series, Kawasaski drew another base on balls and again greeted Lind enthusiastically. The refreshing newcomer turned Lind into an instant fan.

"I said to myself, 'That's my favorite player in the big leagues,'" Lind recalls. "And here he is on my team now."

* * * *

The very first time that Munenori played in front of a home crowd at Rogers Centre, he made an impression. Playing against the Chicago White Sox in an early season game in 2013, he tripled to the gap in left field and flashed some serious leather at shortstop, turning a flashy double play to quell a White Sox uprising. His antics and zest for the game had the crowd chanting:

"Ka-WAhhhh-zak-EEEE. Ka-Wahhhh-zak-EEE."

* * * *

It was a serious foot injury to star shortstop Jose Reyes that gave Kawasaki his chance and he was making the most of it.

"He's a special guy," John Gibbons said after a game. "He's got an infectious personality. The players all have fun with him. In the dugout we don't necessarily know what he's saying but he's fun listening to." He added, "It's no wonder the fans love him."

* * * *

Adam Lind paid a special tribute to Munenori Kawasaki. Soon after Kawasaki had beaten the Atlanta Braves with a walk-off double in 2013, he went to an Atlanta clothing store and bought out their stock of tank top shirts depicting the Japanese rising sun and with the words JAPAN printed across the chest. He then distributed the shirts to teammates who grabbed them like adolescent girls attacking merchandise at a Justin Bieber concert.

* * * *

Kawasaki has become so popular in Toronto that in June of 2013 a group of fans mounted a write-in campaign to send him to the all-star game. At the time, his average was a paltry .207 and his on-base percentage an unimpressive .322. He had no home runs and only five extra base hits. But the replacement for injured shortstop Jose Reyes was leading the American League in personality. Check that … actually he was leading both leagues in personality.

* * * *

All good things must come to an end and so it was on June 25, 2013, when manager John Gibbons took the rare step of calling a clubhouse meeting to announce that Kawasaki was being sent down to Triple A Buffalo to make room for returning superstar Jose Reyes. Usually such formal announcements are reserved for departing superstars, not .225 hitting utility players with a single, albeit city-stirring homer. Pitcher Mark Buehrle, fresh from a 5-1 loss to Tampa Bay, expressed the thoughts of many when he said, "This is the part of the game that sucks. The fans and the guys in here basically fell in love with this guy. I love the guy. After the game, Gibby (Blue Jays manager John Gibbons) called us together to tell us he was getting sent down. I don't think I've ever seen that before. Usually you come in the next day and see the empty locker and that's how you find out a guy got sent down."

* * * *

As for Kawasaki, he received the news with the kind of attitude that, in record time, had endeared him to Toronto fans. Speaking through an interpreter, he said, "These were the best fans and the best teammates. For two months it's been an incredible experience for me. I appreciate everybody from the fans and the players who helped me through it." He went on to say, "I absolutely can't believe how I have been accepted by the players and the fans. For this one strange Japanese guy to come here and be accepted the way I have is unbelievable."

In typical Munenori fashion, he added a touch of levity, as much for his down-at-the-mouth supporters as for himself: "It's not as if I've died. I'm still a baseball player. It's just that tomorrow the field will be different, but I'm still around and ready to help the team when they need it. It's been a terrific experience. I really appreciate everybody and I love everybody."

Kawasaki reminded everyone that despite high power agents and multimillion dollar contracts, baseball is still just a game. A game that Kawasaki played with the unfettered joy of a sandlot player.

"What I'll remember most about Munenori—among an assortment of other things—is that when the Blue Jays had that 11-game winning streak, he was there starting every day," Jerry Howarth said. "Every day! He was a big part of that when injuries sidelined Jose Reyes. Munenori had played over 75 games at that point and the Blue Jays were above .500 with him and under .500 in the games he didn't play. That tells you a lot about his contribution."

Jimmy Key

Control. That was what defined the career of Jimmy Key. It's what kept him in the Majors for fifteen seasons and what made him one of the most respected pitchers in the game. The southpaw possessed just an average fastball but could paint the plate with the touch of a true artist, a master of his craft. He kept hitters off balance and confused. That's why he was called "the thinking man's pitcher."

No less an authority than the great Ted Williams admired the Blue Jays mound magician. In 1995, Williams was interviewed for the book *Ted Williams' Hit List*. When asked about what kinds of pitchers gave him the most trouble, the last man to bat .400 for an entire season singled out Bob Feller, who was the best fastball pitcher of his time. But he said that the toughest pitchers were the smartest pitchers, guys like Whitey Ford, Bob Lemon, Spud Chandler, Dick Donovan, and Hoyt Wilhelm.

"Those kinds of pitchers are still around today and still darn successful," he said. "Smart, crafty guys like Jimmy Key. Key looks real good to me. He would have been tough on me. He's a left-hander and he's got a good delivery—a tough, high, three-quarter delivery." Receiving such praise from the likes of Teddy Ballgame has to be akin to winning a Cy Young Award.

* * * *

For eight seasons, starting in 1985, Key was an integral part of the Toronto rotation.

Although statistically not his best season, Key came through in the 1992 postseason when he helped pitch the Jays to their first World Series title. He notched two wins during that historic Series and posted an ERA that at first glance looks like a misprint—1.00. It was fitting that the last game he pitched as a member of the Toronto Blue Jays was the win that clinched their first World Series.

BILLY KOCH

The Jays selected Koch fourth overall in the 1996 draft. He made his major league debut with the club on May 5, 1999, and soon took over the closer role from Graeme Lloyd. His rookie year was a triumph. He rang up 31 saves and posted a 3.39 ERA while receiving some modest consideration for AL Rookie of the Year. He also set the Jays record for saves by a first year player.

He upped his save total to 33 in 2000, and to 36 in 2001. Newly minted GM J. P. Ricciardi then decided to cash in on his value and dealt him as part of a rebuilding phase. He was shipped to Oakland for Justin Miller and Eric Hinske. He responded to the trade by winning the Rolaids Relief Man of the Year on the strength of 44 saves in 50 opportunities. After stops in Oakland and Florida, he was signed to a one-year deal and brought back to the Blue Jays in time for 2005 spring training in hopes of bolstering the Jays pen. That was as far as he got. With an ERA as high as his socks (15.00), he was released.

DENNIS LAMP

His career record of 96-96, spread over 19 seasons and several major league teams, does not suggest perfection. In fact, taken in isolation, Dennis Lamp's career numbers all but define mediocrity. His lifetime ERA of 3.93 is certainly respectable, but far from exceptional. He does appear in the record books, but only as the supporting cast in a pair of significant achievements by more heralded stars. He gave up future Hall of Famer Lou Brocks's 3000th hit and also future Hall of Famer Cal Ripken Jr.'s first major league hit. Something to tell the grandkids for sure, but only as the lead-in to this: In 1985, Dennis Lamp went

11-0 for the Toronto Blue Jays as a full-time reliever. That's a 1.000 winning percentage for those scoring at home. His ERA was 3.32 in 53 appearances, 105.2 innings of work. He fashioned a 1.16 WHIP and struck out 68 batters. More importantly, he was instrumental in leading the Jays to their first-ever playoff appearance.

He continued to excel in the postseason, appearing in 3 games in the ALCS against Kansas City and pitching a total of 9.1 innings of scoreless ball. He gave up only two hits in that span, walked one, and struck out 10. His WHIP was a microscopic 0.32. When the MVP votes were cast, Lamp finished 21st. Not a bad story to tell the grandkids. Not bad at all.

BRETT LAWRIE

B rett Lawrie grew up in a household that was basically hockey free. "Hockey was never an option for me growing up," Lawrie admitted in 2009. "We were a baseball household, and I found other sports to play during hockey season, like basketball." The irony here is that Lawrie has a hockey mentality. He plays the game with an aggressiveness that any NHL coach would kill for. Think Brad Marchand. He attacks the ball as if he were about to take a slap shot. At the hot corner, he has the reflexes of a goalie. He runs the basepaths as if he had a breakaway with an opponent in hot pursuit. And you can bet that if baseball had a penalty box, Brett would have spent some time there. He is intense. He celebrates hits as if he just scored the winning goal in OT. Homers get the full treatment—including injury-inducing high fives with teammates.

Brett Lawrie arrived on the Major League baseball scene with all the subtlety of a tsunami. In 2011, at the age of 21, he had 9 home runs and slugged at a .580 pace in only 43 games (a mere

150 at-bats). The performance had Blue Jay Nation abuzz, as much for his all-out approach to the game as for the number he posted. At *bluebirdbanter.com* Tom Dakers suggested that, "Brett has some maturing to do, and he runs the bases like he doesn't understand that the other team can tag him out." In other words, his strength was also his weakness. After his meteoric rise, he fell back to earth in 2012, playing 125 games and batting a pedestrian .273 with 11 homers.

But the real fear is that the third baseman plays with such intensity he is in danger of flaming out, or at least, burning out. Entering the 2013 campaign, manager John Gibbons was reluctant to rein in the young Canadian prodigy. "I'm not going to tell him to back off because that's what got him here," said Gibbons. "That's what put him on the map as an amateur. Three or four years from now, I'm sure he'll slow down a bit, but intensity is a big part of this business. Guys that have it, who can bring it every day, are often your better players."

* * * *

Well known for his mid-game ejections, when Lawrie was called out on strikes by umpire Dan Bellino in the bottom of the third inning of a May 24, 2013, game against the Baltimore Orioles, he flipped his bat, slam-dunked his helmet, and tossed his batting gloves aside in disgust. For this triple crown of disrespect, he was immediately ejected by Bellino, who also banished manager John Gibbons when he rushed to his hitter's defense. Crew chief Wally Bell later told reporters that it was the jettisoning of his batting gloves that prompted his heave-ho. It "wasn't etiquette in baseball," he said.

"Next time he's got to throw his gloves in the other direction, I guess," Gibbons told reporters after the game.

* * * *

One of Lawrie's best friends on the Blue Jays was J. P. Arencibia (now a Florida Marlin). Asked to describe Lawrie, the catcher summed him up thusly: "Can't sit still and only talks in movie quotes."

Luis Leal

Amateur free agent Luis Leal signed with the Blue Jays before the 1979 season. The right-handed reliever played in Toronto from 1980 to 1985. In 1984 he won 13 games and lost 8 while compiling a 3.89 ERA and 134 strikeouts.

Luis Leal has the distiction of being the opposing pitcher for the Toronto Blue Jays on May 15, 1981, when Cleveland's Len Barker spun a perfect game for the Indians.

* * * *

On June 2, 1984, at Exhibition Stadium in Toronto, visiting Yankees manager Yogi Berra attempted to torpedo Blue Jays starter Luis Leal by having two massive submarine sandwiches delivered to him before the game. Berra had an insider tip that Leal was a sucker for fast food. A delegation from Mr. Submarine arrived on the mound just before the game was to begin. It was left to Cito Gaston to remove the 6' deli distraction from the field. The pickle alone would have fed the Blue Jays infield. Yogi's effort failed. Although Leal departed after four innings, the Blue Jays still won the game 9-8. The Jays ended up using the two semi-subversive subs as a postgame victory feast.

AL LEITER

"Al just always has fun. He's kind of rambunctious but at the same time very loyal to the game," Jerry Howarth said. "He puts everything he has into everything he does, first pitching and now broadcasting, where he really does his homework. He's a big picture guy and in '92 got a World Series ring for having pitched in one game. That alone doesn't mean a lot but then he was a key part of the '93 team, both as a starter and as a reliever. That made both rings very important to him."

ADAM LIND

Adam Lind came to the Blue Jays for a brief cup of coffee in September of 2006. In April of the following year he was called up from Syracuse to fill in for the injured Reed Johnson and remained until Johnson recovered in early July, then he was sent back to the farm. In that short stint he hit 11 homers and added 48 RBI and his appetite for the big leagues had been whetted. After another failed start in 2008, he was brought back to the big club for good on June 21st, finishing the year with 9 homers and 40 RBI.

Lind's breakthrough came in 2009 as he became the Jays' new designated hitter. He responded to the new assignment by driving in a record six runs on Opening Day in a 12-5 win over the Detroit Tigers. He continued the offensive assault with 11 RBI in five games, matching the mark set eight years earlier by Carlos Delgado. The hot start continued throughout the season and when the final stats were compiled, they showed that he had struck for 179 hits, including 30 home runs, 114 RBI, and a .305 batting average.

Lind really broke loose against the Boston Red Sox on September 29, hitting three homers. An early Christmas present came on December 15th of that year, as he was presented with the Edgar Martinez Award as the best DH in baseball.

"Adam worked on his hitting more than anyone," Matt Stairs said. "The man loved to hit! And he knew his role in the bigs was going to be to hit. So he spent a lot of time on hitting. Then they had to work on his defense to bring that up to code. The bottom line is that if you put him in the middle of the lineup, he would automatically make your team a lot stronger."

JESSE LITSCH

"Litsch enjoyed the game. Unfortunately, he got hurt," Matt Stairs explained. "He came up and pitched well in his first game against Baltimore and got a win. Jesse was always picking your brain. He wanted to know what was going on. Marcum and A. J. and those guys used to talk to him quite a bit about pitching and what to throw in certain situations. He was willing to learn."

DAVE LEMANCZYK

Pitcher Dave Lemanczyk was an original member of the Blue Jays when they made their debut on Opening Day in 1977. Two days later Lemanczyk pitched the first complete game in franchise history, as the Jays lost 3-2 to the Chicago White Sox.

* * * *

Lemanczyk made Blue Jays history again when he initiated three double plays in a single game against the Red Sox in September of '77.

CANDY MALDONADO

As the Toronto Blue Jays battled to the 1992 pennant in pursuit of their first World Series title, they had many detractors and doubters more than ready to remind them of their past playoff record of disappointing losses.

"If I was living in the past, my grandmother would still be alive," said outfielder Candy Maldonado. "The past is in the past." He was proven right, as the Jays went all the way and brought Canada its first World Series championship.

SHAUN MARCUM

"Shaun Marcum was a nut. In a good way," Matt Stairs described. "If there's a single player I've played with in the major and minor leagues who was a happy-go-lucky, nothing-bothers-you, enjoy-the-game, enjoy-the-moment guy, it would be Shaun Marcum. He didn't let too many things bother him. Deep down inside he might have, but he covered it up pretty well. He enjoyed it, he loved pitching. He wanted to pitch, and he's still doing well with that devastating changeup of his. It's nice to see."

BUCK MARTINEZ

Baseball fans know Buck Martinez as one of the most respected and authoritative announcers in the game. As a former Major League catcher and manager, he brings a combination of experience and expertise to the mic. He talks inside baseball and strategy and backs it up with anecdotes from his own days behind the plate.

* * * *

It's hardly surprising that one of the most legendary Canadian stories of courage and dedication in sport involves a hockey player. In Game Six of the 1964 Stanley Cup finals, Bobby Baun's ankle was broken by a Gordie Howe slap shot. He was carried off the ice on a stretcher, his season at an end. Or so it seemed. To the surprise of everyone, he returned to the ice, having refused treatment from the doctor and scored the winning goal in overtime. The Leafs went on to win the Stanley Cup and Baun was an instant legend.

Needless to say, Baun's courage has entered Toronto sports lore.

But there was another guy who also risked his career by playing after an injury. Buck Martinez. It's not often that you hear a double play described as heroic; slick, sure, smooth, yes, but heroic? Well, this one was.

Just days before the 1985 All-Star Game, the Blue Jays were playing the Mariners in Seattle. With Phil Bradley on second, Gorman Thomas singled to right. The throw from right fielder Jesse Barfield unleashed a great throw to home plate, where Martinez was waiting. The ball arrived in time and the catcher stood in front of him to make the tag. Somehow Buck managed to hold onto the ball during the resulting collision, but the impact tore ligaments in his ankle and his leg formed a pretzel under him at an unnatural angle.

Blue Jays starter Tom Filer, who was backing up the play, approached to render assistance to the fallen player who was in obvious distress. But the umpire had not called time and Thomas tried to take third. Martinez rose Lazarus-like from the ground and threw to third. The ball took off and ended up in shallow left, where George Bell fielded it and threw toward the plate, where Thomas was now heading at full speed. Martinez caught the throw and tagged the runner out. It was a bizarre 9-2-7-2 double play—one for the books! Martinez was taken off the field in a stretcher and missed the rest of the season.

"One of the greatest plays in the history of baseball," Jerry Howarth praised. "Once again, it just shows the grit and determination of Buck Martinez."

* * * *

When Martinez left the broadcast booth after 14 years in 2001 to take over as manager of the Blue Jays, he talked about the importance of keeping his players on an even keel. "I've talked to the team about staying calm," he said in a *Sports Illustrated* article. "You don't want to see the pilot walk out of the cockpit and ask, 'Jeez, what the hell is going on?' We may be going to hell in a handbasket, but I'll be cool about it."

Martinez served as manager in 2001 and part of 2002, before he was fired midway through the season.

The Mascots

The first Blue Jays mascot was B. J. Birdy. He ruled the roost from 1979 to 1999, before being knocked off his perch by Ace and Diamond. Today, Ace rules the roost.

BOBBY MATTICK

It's a good thing that former Jays manager Bobby Mattick chose a career in baseball instead of becoming a motivational speaker. During spring training of 1981, Jim Clancy was struggling on the mound and Kenny Schrom was itching for his chance to show what he could do as a reliever. Mattick saw the eagerness in the young man and put his hand on his shoulder. "Son," he said, "I'd really like to put you in this game, but we're trying to win it."

JOHN MAYBERRY

In 1980, John (Big John) Mayberry became the first Toronto Blue Jay to reach the 30-homer plateau.

Mayberry also played a pivotal role in the Blue Jays' first triple play. It was April 22, 1978, and a sellout crowd at Exhibition Stadium was enjoying the game between the Jays and the visiting Chicago White Sox. With runners on first and second, Jays starter Jim Clancy was pitching to Junior Moore. Moore got the bunt sign from the third base coach and attempted to advance the runners into scoring position. He failed to get the bat on top of the ball and popped it up. Clancy charged from the mound and made the catch, then turned and threw the ball to Mayberry at first for the second out. Seeing the lead runner was caught in no man's land between second and third, Mayberry alertly rifled the ball to shortstop Luis Gomez, who was covering second, for the third out. Triple play. The crowd, which included then-Canadian Prime Minister Pierre Trudeau, went wild.

* * * *

Mayberry was a well-liked teammate who went out of his way to make players feel welcome, at least up to a point. Rookie Paul Hodgson remembers his introduction to Big John during spring training. "You'd come to the ballpark in the mornings and see which split squad you were on that day. Typically the vets would stay home, play two or three innings, and then go fishing or golfing. The kids were put on the bus and sent to Fort Myers or some horrible place, and so every morning players would come to look at the list on the wall. And there was John Mayberry, sitting right next to it. Any unfortunate rookie who went to the list had to confront John, waiting there with a cup of coffee and a cigarette in his hand. He'd growl, 'Don't even check the board, kid. Just get your stuff and get on the bus.' That was Big John."

On the flip side, Hodgson also explained, "Today some players are 'brands' and the rest of the team has to put up with all of that. In our day no one was a brand. Mayberry signed a big deal for $800,000, so he got teased for having the 'big pack.' Well, that's chump change today. John was great for the organization, great for inspiring the love of baseball in Toronto. The fans worshipped him."

JOHN McDONALD

Whatever else it may have been, it will never be called the pride of the Yankees. To some it may seem like a trivial incident, childish even, but to baseball purists that's the point. It was May 30, 2007, and the Blue Jays were hosting the storied franchise of Ruth, Gehrig, DiMaggio, Mantle, and most currently Jeter. The Yankees were leading by two runs in the top of the ninth and looking to expand their lead. They had runners on second and third with two out and Jorge Posada at the plate. Posada swung mightily and hit a high fly ball toward third base.

Third baseman Howie Clark camped under the routine fly and waited for it to settle into his glove for the third out.

Suddenly, inexplicably, he moved aside, and the ball fell to the ground. The lead runner scored, and A-Rod was standing on third with a smug grin on his face. Suddenly, all hell broke loose. John McDonald made a move to go after Rodriguez and was stopped by the umpiring crew. Other Blue Jays expressed their outrage verbally.

As A-Rod passed Clark in the base path he had seemed to have yelled some variant of "Mine!" effectively calling Clark off the ball. Naturally, the third baseman thought the voice was that of shortstop McDonald. Except it wasn't John McDonald at all. It was Alex Rodriguez.

The next Yankees batter, Jason Giambi, singled in two more runs, and any chance of a last-inning comeback by the Jays was gone.

After the game, the Jays were still incensed, no one more so than manager John Gibbons.

"I haven't been in the game that long," he said with sarcasm. "Maybe I'm naïve. But, to me, it's bush league. One thing, to everybody in this business, you always look at the Yankees, and they do things right. They play hard, class operation, that's what the Yanks are known for. That's not Yankee baseball."

Third base coach Larry Bowa was one of the few pinstripers to come to A-Rod's defense. "If you say, 'I got it,' I think that's very unacceptable," he said. "He didn't say, 'I got it.' He said, 'Hey, hey.' They parted like the Red Sea."

* * * *

The incident didn't stop there. When the two teams met next time in Toronto, Jays pitcher Josh Towers hit A-Rod with a pitch in the shin (to some, it appeared that they had tried unsuccessfully to hit him the previous night as well).

Although he wasn't playing that day, Matt Stairs had more than a front-row seat. "I think a lot of people don't realize why I was pissed off, and a lot of guys were pissed off over the thing," he explains. "It wasn't that it was fly ball and that A-Rod yelled 'Boo' or whatever he said to Clark at third base. It was more the fact that when John McDonald said something to him, A-Rod turned to him and goes, 'Well, who the f are you?' You know? And disrespecting another player is where I took offense, and that's what pissed me off and that's why what happened happened."

What happened was that the very able-bodied and very loyal Stairs was having it out with the high-priced Yankee star.

"You respect all the Major League ballplayers, and unfortunately there are guys in baseball who think they're better than anyone else...," Stairs said. "When someone else is doing well, they want to get the limelight back on themselves."

FRED McGRIFF

Before the 1983 season, the Blue Jays and Yankees announced a trade. The Jays would send catcher Tom Dodd and reliever Dale Murray to the Yankees for outfielder Dave Collins and pitcher Mike Morgan. Collins was the key person for the Jays but Pat Gillick also asked that New York throw in a first baseman they had drafted in the ninth round, the 233rd overall pick. At the time, the move was scarcely noticed by anyone outside the Jays front office. In short, he was a throw-in.

There was no doubt that the player in question, Fred McGriff, was a work in progress, a long shot. He had undoubted home run potential but lacked discipline at the plate and had yet to figure out minor league, let alone major league, pitching. Thus began his odyssey from one minor league encampment to the next. He showed improvement at every stop and was invited to the Blue Jays spring training in 1984.

His first turn in the batting cage was a revelation. He was hitting the ball with authority, and Blue Jay regulars had gathered to admire the long bombs he was launching into the stratosphere at the Englebert Complex in Dunedin. Dave Collins was among those watching this coming-out party for an emerging young talent.

"I'd just like to know one thing," he said. "Which one of us was the throw-in?"

It wasn't until 1987 that McGriff finally stuck with the parent club, but once there, he wasn't to be moved.

"To me, Fred is very close to being a Hall of Famer too, even though he's overshadowed by others who got into the game in a different way and performed differently," Jerry Howarth said. "Fred's overall abilities as a player and a hitter were just outstanding. He may be the most modest guy around, with so many great accomplishments. He is so understated and shy in his personality—more outgoing now that the years have gone by though. He's a coach and he's a student of the game and passes on his information and experience in his humble way."

* * * *

When the left-handed hitting McGriff came to the Jays, he was often platooned and used only against right-handed pitchers. There is no doubt that he was susceptible to southpaws with good curveballs. The Blue Jays, under managers Bobby Cox and Jimy Williams, certainly had enough left-right platoons in the mid-eighties, including Dave Collins (L) and Jesse Barfield (R), Garth Iorg (L) and Rance Mulliniks (R), Cliff Johnson (L) and George Orta (R), Buck Martinez (L) (and later leftie Pat Borders) and Ernie Whitt (R).

Fred McGriff's right-handed DH counterpart was Cecil Fielder. Some pairings worked better than others.

Dave McKay

The only Canadian in the lineup when the Blue Jays played their first game on April 7, 1977, was Dave McKay. The Vancouver native chipped in with two singles as the Jays beat the White Sox 9-5.

Randy Moffitt

Despite a respectable 12-year career as a Major League pitcher, Randy Moffitt is more famous for being the brother of tennis superstar Billie Jean (Moffitt) King. His stay in Toronto fell at the very end of that career. He posted a 6-2 record with 10 saves and an ERA of 3.77.

Paul Molitor

Readers of a certain age will remember the classic TV Western *Gunsmoke* starring James Arness as Dodge City marshal Matt Dillon. Dillon was a quiet hero who let his actions speak for him. He didn't seek the limelight and it was usually the supporting cast, often his sidekick—first Chester and later Festus—who would maintain law and order in Dodge while he was out of town. Often he appeared only at the end of the episode, riding into Dodge just in time to sort out the bad guys and restore peace and relative tranquility to his frontier town. Paul Molitor was Toronto's Matt Dillon. He came to town to contribute to the team, but when the going got tough, he stepped up and handled the situation.

"He had that sixth sense for the game, like Roberto Alomar and Willie Mays and Paul could just think things through in a very quick moment and make adjustments—and share those moments with his teammates, which was admirable because he too was such a good team player. Individually he obviously stood out, he's a Hall of Famer, but he would share experiences with his team and his younger players and teammates to make them better because he knew that would make the team better," Jerry Howarth said.

Was there ever a better situational Blue Jay hitter than Paul Molitor? If you need reminding, think back to the ninth inning of Game Six of the 1993 World Series. The Blue Jays trailed by a run with Mitch "Wild Thing" Williams pitching for the Phillies. Rickey Henderson was on first base and Devon White was at the plate, while Molitor kneeled in the on-deck circle. Joe Carter, the man who with a single swing of the bat would soon be a Canadian hero, was in the hole. Molitor later revealed to *Sports Illustrated*'s Tom Verducci that his thinking process went something like this:

If Devon White makes an out, I know if I hit a home run, I will live every boy's dream about hitting a home run that wins the World Series. When Devon White did, indeed, make an out, Molitor's thinking changed to the strategic rather than the dramatic. "To fight that thinking was probably the most difficult part of that at-bat. And going up I was, like, 1 for 8 against Mitch. So for me looking to be a hero didn't make sense. I just tried to keep the line moving."

It was the right decision at the right time, arrived at for all the right reasons. When Williams delivered an inside fastball, Molitor was ready. Instead of trying to pull the pitch over the left field wall, he lined the pitch into center field. The characteristically unselfish play allowed Joe Carter to become an instant hero across Canada, but real fans know that without Molitor, there might have been no heroics at all.

* * * *

A *SI* piece by Tom Verducci, entitled "The Best," examined which major leaguers did "the little things" best. One of the categories was clutch hitting, and not surprisingly the best proponent of that skill was Paul Molitor. That legendary judge of baseball talent Billy Beane, then assistant general manager of the Oakland A's, summed up Molitor's credentials: "Simply put, he's a great hitter in any situation. And with the game on the line, what he does is magnified."

* * * *

Ron Darling, pitcher for the Oakland A's, once compared pitching to Molitor to playing chess against Boris Spassky. "It's a match of wits and you can't help but feel he's one move ahead of you." Molitor disagreed. "It's not so much a chess game as it is cribbage," he said. "And I'm going to peg you to death."

* * * *

Molitor came to Toronto to replace Dave Winfield, who had moved on to New York, for the 1993 season. The soon-to-be Hall of Famer did not disappoint. He had 211 hits and 22 homers, while batting .332 and driving in 111 runs. Moreover, his steady presence kept the Jays on an even keel throughout the season. For his exploits in the World Series that year, where he batted an even .500 (12 for 24), he was rewarded with the series MVP award.

* * * *

Molitor was known to his teammates as "Molly" or "Paulie." Because of his skills as a leadoff hitter, the press dubbed him "The Ignitor," a moniker that he disliked intensely. "Aside from the fact that it's not even spelled right (Ed. Note: to rhyme with Molitor), it's a terrible nickname," he once said. "I never once entered a room and my friends said, 'Hey, it's the Ignitor!'"

* * * *

When Molitor came to the Jays in 1993 after fourteen years as a member of the Milwaukee Brewers, he had to choose a uniform number. He had worn # 4 for his entire major league career, from 1978-1992. Asked if he would keep that number, he quipped, "Is that Canadian or American? Maybe it will turn out to be a 3."

Since the number 4 was already being used by veteran Alfredo Griffin, Molitor selected number 19 instead. He did it as a tribute to his best friend on the Brewers, Robin Yount (when Molitor left Toronto for the Minnesota Twins after his 3-year contract had expired, he again donned his familiar number 4). His respect and affection for his longtime teammate was genuine and deep. The Brewers were now a young team, and Yount was practically a senior citizen among kids. Molitor worried about his old comrade. "Robin just doesn't know a lot of guys on the team and I worry about that," he admitted. "I mean, who's he going to eat breakfast with on the road?"

* * * *

As a player, Molitor was a "glass is half full" kind of guy. "That's one good thing about baseball," he once said. "You always get another chance. In baseball, you get 600 chances a year."

* * * *

It was late September of 1993, and the Blue Jays were on the verge of clinching the American League East title. There was more than a little irony in the fact that his new team was poised to clinch in a September 27 game in Milwaukee, where Molitor had built his legend. "I won't get any special satisfaction out of it," he said on the eve of the 3-game series. "I don't think there's a bad place to win a division title. I've been waiting a long time to do it, so they're all good." He then added, "Winning in Milwaukee will be a little awkward, though."

The awkwardness did not extend to his swing. In the second inning, on the very first pitch of his first at-bat, he swung smoothly and jerked the pitch over the left-field fence. The final score in the rain-shortened contest was 2-0, and Molitor had provided the winning margin.

* * * *

The deal for Molitor had paid off big. He had contributed mightily to the Jays' amazing regular season. He batted .332, good for second-best in the AL. Only teammate John Olerud's .363 mark was higher (Olerud, Molitor, and Roberto Alomar (.326) finished one-two-three in the batting race, the first time this had happened to three players from the same team in 100 years). He drove in 111 runs and compiled 211 hits, most in the junior circuit. He crossed home plate 121 times, tops on the Jays. At the ripe old baseball age of 37, the Ignitor still had some spring in his legs as well. He stole 22 bases, admittedly more on smarts than speed. And to top it all off, he showed some newfound power, hitting 22 homers. It was the first time in his long career that he had gone deep as many as 20 times. "That was a big surprise, after all those years," he told Rosie DiManno of the *Toronto Star*.

* * * *

Much has been made of the contrasting styles, both literally and baseballically, of the World Series opponent in 1993. The Jays were a buttoned-down, conservative lot, while the Philadelphia Phillies were free spirits, long of hair and short of discipline. It was old school vs new school, and if you had to pick a person who represented both schools of thought, natural choices would be Mitch "Wild Thing" Williams for the Phillies and Paul Molitor of the Blue Jays. Williams's hair was long and disheveled; he was erratic and unpredictable; Molitor's hair was short, combed, and corporate. Molitor joked about the striking differences in the two teams. "I'll bet we have more cellular phones than they do," he said.

* * * *

The World Series presents an annual problem for the winners of the National League and American League pennants. In two letters, that problem is the DH: the American League has one and the National League does not. The MLB brain trust determined that the fairest way to deal with these differing rules was to follow the rules of the home ballpark—in this case, the DH would be in effect in Toronto and not in Philadelphia. For Cito Gaston and the Blue Jays, Paul Molitor's status had to be addressed. Game One and Game Two—and if needed, Games Six and Seven, would be played with the designated hitter rule in effect in Toronto. The problem lay in Games Three, Four, and Five. The options were either to bench the offensive sparkplug of the team or find a place for him at first or third base. The only certainty was that he would not play the outfield. "Unless everyone is dead on this team, Molitor will not play left field," Gaston said.

Gaston would be criticized whatever he decided to do. The decision, when it came, was either courageous or foolhardy, depending on who you talked to: Gaston benched American League batting champ John Olerud and installed Molitor at first. Instead of becoming a contentious issue between two egos, it became a contest of who could be more humble. In one of the unintentionally funniest lines, Molitor said, "John is way past me [in] humbleness. For me, I've learned it." The Jays won in a blowout 10-3, making the point very much moot. Molitor tripled, homered, and chipped in with a single.

* * * *

In Game Four in the City of Brotherly Love, Molitor was moved from first to third, replacing Ed Sprague. Olerud was returned to his rightful spot at first. The challenge of playing the hot corner after all those years was considerable. The last time he had played the position was three years earlier in 1990 when he incurred a shoulder injury. But challenges appealed to Paul Molitor. It was a case of the Jays "winning ugly," but Molitor's play at third did not contribute to the ugliness. It was a 15-14 slugfest and defense was just a rumor. Game Five found Molitor back on third and again he performed his job without incident, although the Phillies prevailed in a pitching duel between Curt Schilling and Juan Guzman. In the two games at third he made only three throws to first, all on the mark. Molitor had not only survived Philadelphia, but in doing so he had met all challenges, at the plate and in the field.

* * * *

It was October 23, 1993, Game Six of the 1993 World Series. The Blue Jays broke in front in the first inning, scoring three runs, one driven in by a Molitor triple and another scored by him on a Joe Carter sac fly. In the fifth inning, Molitor homered, and the chants of "MVP!" rippled throughout the frenzied ballpark. The Phillies responded and carried a 6-5 lead into the bottom of the ninth. The Jays would have to come back against Mitch Williams, the sometimes brilliant, sometimes erratic, closer for the Phils. On this day, he proved to be erratic, walking Rickey Henderson. He then retired Devon White on a fly ball. Molitor then stepped into the batter's box and lined a single to center field. With runners at first and second, Joe Carter attacked a 2-1 pitch and launched it toward the left-field fence. Molitor appeared to be walking on air as he rounded third and crossed home plate. He had his World Series championship and his World Series MVP award.

* * * *

On the field after the win, Molitor wept openly. When asked later whether it was true that he had cried, he said, "I'm not ashamed or embarrassed to admit that."

* * * *

In six World Series games, Molitor had 12 hits in 24 at-bats: 2 doubles, 2 triples, and 2 homers. He scored a total of 10 runs and drove in 8.

* * * *

The World Series championship meant a whole new level of celebrity for Molitor. He was invited to appear on the *David Letterman Show* with Phillies rough-hewn Lenny Dykstra. Letterman, a knowledgeable baseball fan, asked him what it was like to reach first base and socialize with tobacco-chewing free-spirit John Kruk. "Basically," said Molitor, "he tries to convince you, you were lucky to get a hit. And he spits on your shoes a lot."

* * * *

Ted Williams, arguably the greatest hitter who ever lived, had high praise for Molitor. "I watch him and I say to myself, *there is probably the best hitter in the game today,*" said the Kid. But he didn't stop there. "He's the closest thing to Joe DiMaggio in the last 30 years. Matter of fact, every time I watch him I say 'There's Joe!'" To put that in perspective, Teddy Ballgame called DiMaggio "the greatest all-round player I [ever] saw."

* * * *

Asked by ESPN's Jim Caple what song might be played at his Hall of Fame induction, Molitor said, "I guess when you talk about Springsteen lyrics, the theme of 'Glory Days' is the older you get the better you were, so I guess that would be appropriate to play. I'll be able to exaggerate as well as anybody."

* * * *

Molitor's induction into the Baseball Hall of Fame put him in some very exclusive company, including that of a genuine baseball philosopher. "It was unbelievable to be surrounded with those guys [at Cooperstown]," he admitted. "There's a golf tournament every year, and I was playing with Yogi Berra. I got to hear a Yogi-ism live and in person. We got to a green, and Yogi had a 60-footer. When he left it 30 feet short, he said, 'If I woulda hit it harder, I'd have missed it shorter.'"

* * * *

In his *Page 2* column, Bill Simmons asked Molitor if his musical hero Bruce Springsteen would be singing at his Hall of Fame ceremonies. "Oh, sure," he smiled. "He's going to do a special show just for me. No, I don't think so. But I got a nice telegram from him."

Simmons then asked Molitor what he would like his plaque to record. Was it the 3,000 hits? The World Series MVP award? The postseason batting average?

"No, I hope it's more about the way I played and then that there were some things I accomplished. If it tells about intelligence and respect, those things carry a lot more meaning to me than 3,000 hits. Describing the way you go about your job means more to me."

Molitor's Hall of Fame plaque actually reads as follows: "A remarkably consistent contact hitter and aggressive base runner with extraordinary instincts. One of three players with more than 3,000 hits, 600 doubles, and 500 steals. A career .306 hitter. Ranks eighth all-time with 3,319 hits. Hit safely in 39 consecutive games in 1987 for the fifth-longest stretch in modern baseball history. A great clutch performer, as evidenced by his record five hits in Game One of the 1982 World Series for the Brewers, and World Series MVP honors for the Champion Blue Jays in 1993. Elected to seven All-Star teams."

* * * *

In his HOF acceptance speech he said, "The baseball memories are great, but when you think about your career, the people memories are even better."

* * * *

"In Canada, when you say PM, they think of Prime Minister, but now they might start thinking Paul Molitor!" said Tim McCarver, the baseball color man when Molitor captured the World Series MVP award.

* * * *

When he retired from the field, Molitor briefly served as hitting coach for the Seattle Mariners. The advice he imparted was also his hitting credo. "Hitting is a lot about failure," he told Bill Simmons. "And your level of success is tied to how well you handle failure. That takes a strong mind. Anytime you do something that you fail at more than you succeed, you're vulnerable to the fragility of how the mind can wear on you. The challenge is to keep guys in a good frame of mind during those times even when they're getting hits less than 3 out of 10 times."

JACK MORRIS

After the Jays 7-2 Game Five loss to the Atlanta Braves in the 1992 World Series, starter Jack Morris was uncharacteristically chastened. A win in the game would have clinched a World Series title for the Blue Jays and the Jays had forked out a team-record $5 million for him to win games like this. "The Atlanta Braves have won two games and I've pitched them both," he said. "They're in trouble. They're in serious trouble, because I don't pitch again." Morris, who was key to getting the Jays to the postseason, had a terrible Series. His ERA was a horrendous 8.44.

Despite his postseason collapse, the Jays more than go their money's worth out of the veteran. His season record was 21-6, and he carried the team on his back down the stretch.

"Jack was a fierce competitor who wanted the ball for the big game—heck he wanted it for every game," Jerry Howarth said. "He was only interested in winning and winning with a complete game from the first pitch to the last pitch. He was the kind of teammate you wanted to lead and he loved that role. As my partner now on radio, I've found him to be compassionate to understand the game. He knows firsthand how difficult it is to play, so when he broadcasts he does so with a great sense of objectivity and fairness. He's been there on that mound before and knows how difficult it is to pitch. As a pitcher, Jack was all business, and any time you put on the uniform, that business is winning and that's what he was all about."

BRANDON MORROW

Brandon Morrow is a prolific tweeter and some of his tweets are as puzzling and disconcerting as a fastball under the chin.

Here's an example: "Anyone know where to find a goat? We need for … uh … something special before JoJo takes the mound … A chicken may work in a pinch."

* * * *

On August 8, 2010, Brandon Morrow authored one of the most memorable pitching performances in Blue Jays history. Working against the formidable Tampa Bay Rays lineup, Morrow was virtually unhittable, allowing one seeing-eye single past the glove of an infielder in nine innings. He also struck out 17 and made many professional hitters look bad in the process.

LLOYD MOSEBY

The terrific trio of Lloyd Moseby, George Bell, and Jesse Barfield were all born within about a week of each other. Bell entered the world on October 21, 1959. Jesse Barfield followed on October 29, and Lloyd Moseby on November 5. It was a very productive 15-day stretch for the Toronto Blue Jays.

* * * *

Lloyd Moseby joined the Blue Jays in the spring of 1980, at the tender age of 20. He had been highly regarded, drafted second in the 1978 amateur draft straight out of high school. Where many organizations would have kept him in the minors for further maturation and experience, the talent-challenged Jays didn't have that luxury. They decided to let him get some on-the-job training in the Major Leagues.

Not surprisingly, the process took time. It wasn't until his fourth year in the Bigs that he started to figure out big-league pitching. Something clicked, all the hard-earned lessons came together, and he had a great offensive outburst in 1983. He powered 18 homers, batted .315, and plated a franchise-high 104 runs. He also stole 27 bases. He was rewarded with a Silver Slugger Award and even garnered some MVP attention.

The progress continued the following year, as he batted .280, drove in 92 runs, and used his speed to lead the American League in triples. Once again, he was a constant threat on the base paths, stealing 39 bases. Despite a drop in average in 1985, his patience at the plate earned him 76 walks. Once on base, he continued to be a threat to steal, disrupting the routine of pitchers throughout the league, as he nabbed 37. He also contributed 18 home runs. In 1986 he hit 21 homers, added 32 steals, and was named to the AL All-Star team for the first time. He hit another 26 homers in '87 and added 96 RBI.

There was another constant in Moseby, and that was his defensive abilities in center field. With his speed, he could cover a considerable part of the outfield and had a respectable arm.

Injuries took their toll during the next few seasons, and after the 1989 season Moseby became a member of the Detroit Tigers.

The 6' 3" Moseby was known as Shaker, earning the nickname from his considerable abilities on the basketball court.

* * * *

Once, in a game against the Chicago White Sox, Shaker successfully stole second base twice—yes twice—on the same play. On the pitcher's delivery, he broke from first and slid successfully into second base as the catcher's throw went over the infielder's head and into center field. Moseby could have easily gone to third on the miscue; however, crafty Chisox shortstop Ozzie Guillen pretended that the ball had been popped up and called for it. Moseby scrambled back to first to avoid being picked off. The relayed throw to first was also wild, going over the first baseman's head and into the dugout. Moseby once again took off for second, sliding in safely and then standing there with a sheepish grin on his face. Moseby had run 270 feet in order to steal second base—twice.

Lloyd Moseby's place among Blue Jay batting leaders:

Games played: 3rd 1392

At-bats: 2nd 5124

Runs Scored: 2nd 768

Hits: 3rd 1319

Doubles: 4th 292

Triples 2nd 60

Home Runs: 6th 149

RBI: 5th 651

Walks: 547

Stolen Bases: 1st 255

Runs Created: 3rd 745

RANCE MULLINIKS

After playing for the Angels and Royals, Mulliniks was a Toronto Blue Jay from 1982 to 1992. In 1984 he was named to the *Sports Illustrated* Dream Team as the utility player.

* * * *

Rance Mulliniks was once asked what the game of baseball would be like if every player was like Nolan Ryan. "Everyone would love each other," said Mulliniks, "and no one would get a hit."

* * * *

Rance Mulliniks was deceptive. When he came to the plate as a designated hitter, he did not exactly strike fear into the hearts of opposing pitchers. He was no Big Papi Ortiz in stature. And yet he was a legitimate offensive threat.

At third base, he was no Brooks Robinson, and yet he was a decent fielder who led the American League three times (1984, '85, '86) in fielding percentage at the hot corner.

* * * *

Rance played third base for the Jays, sharing the position with Garth Iorg, his best friend on the team. He batted .300 three different times as a Jay and still holds the Blue Jays record for single-season fielding percentage by a third baseman, with a .975 mark. He also owns the franchise record for pinch hits, with 59. He played for the 1992 World Series–champion Jays and was named the utility player on the Jays' 25th anniversary team.

* * * *

Mulliniks teamed with Garth Iorg to provide the Jays with a seamless third base combo—the left-handed Rance and the right-handed Iorg.

Some referred to them as Gance Mullinorg. Two players in one, a platoon that was the equivalent of a switch hitter. Seamless, despite very different styles. They both were line drive hitters and both used the same model bat—a 34-inch, 31-ounce Louisville Slugger.

"Rance was the complete player and then being platooned with Garth Iorg, both of those players got the most out of their abilities and skills, Rance facing right-handed pitching and Garth facing left-handed pitching," Howarth said. "Because they were both so unselfish, when they were asked to leave the game in the third or fourth inning when a pitching change was made, they did that in a very positive way and then rooted for the other. That's what you want—Mullinorg."

The left-right tandem gave manager Bobby Cox the flex-ibility to insert the right player at the right time. "They know me like a book," Cox stated. "I look around when there's a pitching change, and one of them has a bat, waiting for me." Mulliniks explained why the system worked. "We know our roles, and we can't get selfish."

* * * *

Like many future major league ballplayers, ten-year-old Rance Mulliniks learned from the hitter's bible of batting, *The Science of Hitting*, by Ted Williams. The book had been given to young Rance by his father, Harvey.

One of Ted's "golden rules" of hitting was to have a massive influence on Rance all throughout his Major League career. "Get a good pitch to hit and be quick with the hands," became his mantra.

* * * *

He looked more like an accountant than a ballplayer, and like an accountant, he recorded some pretty decent numbers in his time with the Jays. In 11 years as a part-time player, he tallied 204 doubles, 68 homers, and an impressive .280 batting average.

* * * *

Mulliniks was once asked whether graphite or aluminum bats might be superior to those made of wood. "I don't know about bats, but they make great fishing poles," he said.

DIONER NAVARRO

The Blue Jays signed catcher Dioner Navarro to a two-year $8 million deal in December of 2013. Navarro is a well-traveled native of Caracas, Venezuela.

* * * *

Navarro is no stranger to adversity. In September of 2003, on their first wedding anniversary, his wife Sherley suffered a brain aneurysm and wasn't expected to live past September 30. She beat the odds and made a complete recovery. Since then, Navarro has worn #30 to honor her and the miracle of her survival. Dioner also has a son with multicystic dysplastic kidney disease who had to have one kidney removed.

* * * *

Navarro loves animals and owns two birds, two dogs, and a chameleon. The chameleon is especially noteworthy since the backstop has changed uniforms no fewer than seven times during his career. His fashion choices included Yankee pinstripes; Dodger blue; Tampa Bay blue; LA blue a second time; Cincinnati red; Chicago Cub red, white, and blue; and now Blue Jay blue, where he should blend in nicely.

JOSE NUNEZ

Let's talk about disasters. Some are caused by El Nino, others by La Nina. Then there is the disaster caused by a Jose Nunez at-bat.

Jose Nunez was a right-handed pitcher for the Blue Jays from 1987-1989, and while his stay in majors was short, the memories linger. We should preface this account by saying that spring training tales are often embellished. This one is not, nor does it need to be.

In March of 1988, the Blue Jays were playing the Philadelphia Phillies in a spring training game in Clearwater, Florida. Since the exhibition contest was being played in a National League ballpark, the teams were playing without the DH rule. In other words, pitchers had to take their cuts at the plate. Which brings us to Jose Nunez, the Blue Jay pitcher of the day. Not only had Nunez never faced Major League pitching, but he had never had any at-bats in the minors either. He was a hitting virgin.

The Phillies pitcher that day was Kevin Gross, but let's face it, it could have been almost anyone. Nunez strode to the plate trying to imitate the hitters he had previously viewed mostly from the mound. Just as he was settling into the batter's box to hit, umpire Dave Pallone called time and instructed him to remove his warm-up jacket. To the sound of howls from his teammates, he took the walk of shame back to the dugout and deposited his jacket. Confidence only slightly shaken, he then returned to the batter's box and had just started to dig in when the umpire once again interrupted. "Ah, Jose," he said as kindly as possible, "you have the wrong batting helmet." Sure enough, Nunez, a left-handed batter, was wearing a helmet with the protective earflap over the left ear and not the one vulnerable to an errant pitch. The laughter had now turned into guffaws and had spread to all parts of the diamond and the stands. Desperation was setting in for the embattled native of the Dominican Republic. Instead of returning to the dugout a second time, he turned the helmet around and wore it as a catcher would. Pallone told him that this was unacceptable, that he must wear the proper helmet and in the proper frontward way. Again Nunez refused to return to his dugout. Instead, he walked across the plate and took the hitting stance of a right-handed hitter.

At this point the scene had deteriorated to an Abbott and Costello routine. Just as Gross was about to go into his windup, he saw that Nunez was staring toward catcher Lance Parrish, a Major League no-no. "What are you doing?" Parrish asked, reasonably. Nunez was refreshingly frank. "I want to see the signs," he said. "O.K., what pitch do you want?" said Gross. "Fastball," countered Nunez. The fastball was delivered as ordered, and Nunez managed to foul it off. He then politley requested a changeup.

At this point the umpire was doubled over and Parrish was shaking with laughter. Gross was in danger of falling off the mound. Finally, finally, he was able to deliver the pitch, and Nunez mercifully grounded out to shortstop to end one of the most hilariously incompetent at-bats in Major League history.

JOHN OLERUD

While hitting well above .400 in early 1993, John Olerud's batting coach Larry Hisle admitted, "I tell the guys at the start of the year that the less I talk to them, the better they must be hitting. At this rate, John and I might never talk."

* * * *

There is no truth to the rumor that John Olerud rode into Toronto on a horse, tipping his Stetson to the women folk and

AP Photo/Gary Stewart

restoring law and order while saying "Aw shucks" a lot. No, he didn't say that, but he did once say after a great performance, "Geez, I'm just glad to be alive to have this opportunity."

With the superstar's shy, modest ways and tall, clean-cut appearance, he was practically the prototype of a hero. Boastful? Not our John.

And yet he had every reason to be. In 1989, Olerud went directly from Washington State University to the majors without spending a single day in the minor leagues. Once there, he inspired both compliments and awe. *Sports Illustrated* said that his "swing is so sweet it should be poured on pancakes." One of the great hitters of his time, Dave Mattingly was even more complimentary, if imitation really is the sincerest form of flattery. In 1990 the Yankee star confessed that he used Olerud as his cure for a prolonged batting slump. Smooth as a Rolls Royce and as compact as a Smart Car, that was his swing.

* * * *

In high school Olerud was called "Cheetah," for the same reason that bald guys are often called "Curly"—ironically, that is. His lack of speed on the base paths was a source of humor, and in sharp contrast to his bat speed. With a resting heartbeat once measured at 44 beats per minute, he followed that old Zen master, Ted Williams, who said, "Wait and be quick." At the plate he was extremely selective, as was Ted. And like Ted, he was sometimes criticized for being too picky. "I think it's true that sometimes I wait for the perfect pitch and let some good ones go by," he once told *Sports Illustrated.*

* * * *

Playing off Olerud's laid-back attitude, an early '90s radio promo for the Blue Jays featured a phone conversation between Bernie, a Jays employee at spring training in Florida, and a friend back in Toronto. Olerud is nearby, waiting to use the pay phone.

"I've been working on John Olerud's shyness," says the man in Florida. "Getting him to come out of his shell."

"Has it worked?" the friend asks.

"Terrific," Bernie says, and hands the phone to Olerud for confirmation.

"Give us your comments on spring training, how you feel, how the other guys feel, and how you think the team will do this year," says the man in Toronto.

"Great," says Olerud.

"Atta boy, John," says Bernie with a stiff smile. He then turns away and whispers into the phone, "I've still got a little work to do."

* * * *

John Olerud's smooth swing and patience at the plate drew comparisons to Ted Williams, the last man to hit .400 in the Major Leagues. The 6'5" former Blue Jays first baseman batted left-handed, as did Teddy Ballgame, and like Ted he was very selective at the plate. Olerud made his own run at .400. In 1993 he started the season with a blistering .450 in April and was batting over .400 as late as August 24th. He settled for a league-best .363. Typically modest, Olerud credited the artificial turf of the SkyDome for some of his hitting success.

Off the field, Olerud and Ted Williams were polar opposites in demeanor. Terrible Ted was fiery and Olerud was so calm that one wag described him as "just north of comatose." To which writer George Will, an unabashed admirer of the understated star added, "and just south of perfection."

* * * *

"John's so modest," Blue Jays president Paul Beeston once said, "if he hit a home run, he'd apologize for losing the ball. You know, I shouldn't say this, because I don't want to put any pressure on him, but you look at him and wonder if that's what Lou Gehrig was like."

* * * *

John Olerud invited comparisons. For starters, he was compared with Ted Williams, Gary Cooper, and Robert Redford. One real ballplayer, one guy playing a real ballplayer, and a fictional ballplayer. The fictional character was Roy Hobbs in *The Natural*, and Robert Redford used Ted Williams as his touchstone for that role too. His Jays teammates called him Hobbsy, and it wasn't a bad moniker. His story is equally dramatic—some would even say far-fetched. He came back from a life-threatening condition to star in the Major Leagues, all the while maintaining the demeanor of an "aw shucks" cowboy. Tall, clean-cut, and reserved, he was practically the prototype of a hero.

"John survived a brain aneurysm and six hours of surgery and in 1989 in February in Washington State and then has just gone on to have a beautiful life, including being a batting champion in 1993 and hitting .363. John, as quiet as he was, was very professional and took the ups and downs with great equanimity and calmness. He was very mindful of the game and put the game first. In his own quiet way he went about being a student of the game. He always played to his abilities, as hard as he could," Jerry Howarth said.

LYLE OVERBAY

L yle Overbay played for the Blue Jays from 2006-2010, coming over from the Milwaukee Brewers. After his initial season in Toronto during which he hit 22 home runs and batted .312, the easy-going first baseman never really lived up to expectations. His average dropped to .240 the following year as his home run output sagged to 10. The following two seasons were mediocre, and after the 2010 season in which he batted .243, albeit with 20 homers, he was gone.

Former teammate Matt Stairs described Overbay: "The way he played the game, he didn't show the emotions. He might not have showed a lot of so-called energy, but that was the type of person he was. He loves the game and he wanted to win real bad. A very good teammate."

DAN PLESAC

D an Plesac was a hard-throwing left-hander for the Toronto Blue Jays. In a June, 2001 game against the Boston Red Sox in Toronto, Sox switch-hitter Carl Everett came to bat against Plesac in the ninth with the score tied 1-1. Famously eccentric, Everett surprised many by settling into the left batter's box. Why? Batting right-handed the previous night, Everett had not fared well against reliever Plesac, striking out on a steady diet of changeups. "I knew I wasn't going to get anything to drive or get up in the air batting right-handed," he told reporters after the game. He went on to reason that with slugger Manny Ramirez batting behind him, his goal was simply to hit the ball into the gap, allowing Manny a chance to drive him in. The strategy worked better than even he expected. Everett hit a slider for a game-winning homer.

PAUL QUANTRILL

Paul Quantrill hailed from London, Ontario. The right-handed reliever was Mr. Reliable for the Toronto Blue Jays from 1996-2001. In addition to a devastating sinker, his biggest assets were pinpoint control and an uncanny ability to pitch countless innings without apparent adverse effects on his "rubber arm." Besides the Blue Jays, he also pitched for the Red Sox, Phillies, Dodgers, Yankees, Padres, and Marlins.

Quantrill had a unique theory about pitching preparation. "The long toss is far and away the most important drill for strengthening my arm," he once claimed. It obviously worked for him. In 1997, when he became a full-time relief pitcher, he appeared in a then-record 77 games for the Jays and recorded an impressive 1.94 ERA. In '98 he pitched in 82 games and finished with a 2.59 ERA and a tie for most "holds," with 27.

In 1999, to conclusively establish his Canadian credentials, he became the only Major League player in history to miss part of a season due to a broken leg suffered in a snowmobile accident.

In 2001 he made the AL All-Star team, leading the circuit in relief wins with 11 and appearances with 80, while posting a 3.04 ERA. Amazingly, he issued a mere 5 bases on balls in 83 innings of work. In the off-season he was dealt, along with Cesar

Izturis, to the LA Dodgers in exchange for Chad Ricketts and Luke Prokopec.

On June 19, 2010, Quantrill was inducted in the Canadian Baseball Hall of Fame in St. Mary's, Ontario.

COLBY RASMUS

There are sibling rivalries, and then there are sibling rivalries. Usually they involve the older brother giving the younger brother a noogie in the backseat of the family station wagon while on the way to the mall. For the Rasmus brothers, the backseat is a baseball diamond and the noogie is a double to the opposite field.

There have been some impressive brother combos in the majors over the years: the DiMaggio brothers, Joe with the Yankees and Dom with the Red Sox always cheered for the other guy while trying hard to best him. The Alous—Matty, Jesus, and Felipe—were fortunate enough to play for the same team—the SF Giants—at least for part of their careers. So did Hank Aaron and his brother Tommie in Atlanta. So older brother Colby and the younger Cory Rasmus were hardly unique. As kids, they played side by side on the same team, but as they grew and developed, their age difference and developmental rates meant that they would play at different levels.

Most brothers are competitive, but when it is their job at stake it elevates considerably. Talk about bittersweet. That's practically the definition. You help to win the game for your team by hitting a home run and a two-bagger. But when the double comes against your little brother, a reliever for the Atlanta Braves just 10 days into his major league career, things change. Colby, in his second full season with the Jays, turned around a 95 mile-per-hour fastball and laced it to the opposite field. It would have been the perfect opportunity for Colby to break into a "2b or not 2b" soliloquy. It was the first time the two had played against each other.

"It was a strange feeling," the elder Rasmus said after the game. "Lot of emotions going on. But it was awesome and terrible at the same time."

In just his second major league appearance, Cory lasted just two innings. He was ultimately done in by a three-run homer off the bat of Edwin Encarnacion, as the Jays romped to a 9-3 win.

Colby even felt conflicted about the Encarnacion homer. "I'm not gonna lie," he admitted. "Definitely my gut kind of wrenched up a little bit. But that's the game."

As for Cory, he was philosophical, as younger brothers often have to be to survive. "It was still awesome," he said later. "Me facing him—that was a lot of fun. It just sucks that he got a hit."

And if you think that his brother was the only family member conflicted, think again.

Their father, Tony Rasmus, and another brother, Cyle, were watching from the stands (he also has a third brother, Casey). Tony had taught them everything about the game of baseball. And he was a tough task master—like the mother who insisted her son play the violin while the other kids were outside playing baseball—except in reverse. He did it for all the right reasons—to help them reach their potential in the game they all loved. But, like the violin mother, he was sometimes criticized for living vicariously through his boys.

"I'm not gonna know what to say, you know what I'm saying?" said the proud father just after the game. "Hang with 'em. That's just the way the game works."

As for the brothers, they thank their dad for the end result, if not for the grinding work involved in making them winners.

"There is no chance we would be here without him," Colby said. "He spent hours throwing to us and hitting us ground balls. I don't even know how many hours."

As for the Braves' manager Fredi Gonzalez, he had no such Smothers Brothers–style angst about who his favorite brother is. "I was hoping our brother would get the better end of that one, but he didn't," Gonzalez said.

As for Colby and Cory, they planned to get together for dinner after the game.

If fate hadn't intervened, the pitcher-batter confrontation might have been reversed. At one time Cory was a much better hitter and Colby a superior pitcher. "Colby couldn't dream to hit like him," recalled the father. An injury to Cory put an end to his hitting career.

JOSE REYES

It shouldn't come as a surprise to anyone that shortstop Jose Reyes is a musician. Some have even gone so far as to call him "Bob Marley with a bat." The native of the Dominican Republic was the National League batting champion in 2011 for the NY Mets. But he's a virtuoso on the base paths too. He topped the National League in steals from 2005-07. He's not bad with the glove, either. In short, the switch-hitting shortstop can play.

His reggae music may seem to be a better fit in the heat of Miami than in Toronto, but Jose Reyes's stay there ended on a very discordant note. During the off-season prior to the 2012 campaign, the Miami Marlins had signed Reyes to a $106 million deal. So for him to be traded a year later to a team in another country and another league was, to say the least, a shock of major league proportions.

"I was shocked, because [Florida Marlins' owner] Jeffrey Loria, he always told me he's never going to trade me," said Reyes at the Toronto press conference announcing his trade to the Jays. "He always called my agent and said, 'Tell Jose to get a good place here to live.'" Only a few days before the blockbuster trade, Loria had again reassured the Dominican shortstop, and according to Reyes had even encouraged him to "get a nice house in Miami."

* * * *

The warmth of the reception he received from Toronto fans soon helped to ease the blow. Reyes discovered a vibrant Caribbean culture within the city known for its diversity.

His musical genre is reggaeton, a fusion of reggae and hip-hop. His song "No Hay Amigo" ("There Is No Friend") promotes the rewards of hard work.

"The song is a message for the children that when I was younger I didn't have anything, but I kept working, and now I have what I have," he has said. He stressed that the music was only a hobby. Baseball was still #1. His former Mets teammates liked the song.

Said outfielder Willie Harris: "I think it's cool as hell. He can hit triples and then rap. Come on, man, a lot of people can't do that."

* * * *

After Jose Reyes came to the Blue Jays from Miami as part of a much-hyped deal, the Jays got off to a less-than-impressive 2-4 start to the 2012 season. Even though Reyes was the only Jays newcomer who was pulling his offensive weight at the time, he defended his teammates. "We expected to be winning this season when we were in Dunedin," he told reporters. "We expected to be winning when we left Florida. We're going to turn this around. We're not playing like we can. I'm not worried. If this was August and we had the same mark [.286 win %] I'd be worried. It's seven games." Then he added with a laugh, "Could we beat this year's Miami Marlins? Of course we could."

* * * *

One of the most painfully embarrassing things for a base runner is to be picked off. It's like going to work and realizing that you forgot to wear pants. The other is to dive safely back to the bag and be hit with a baseball on the fly in the fly. On Sunday, July 21, 2013, at Rogers Centre, this happened to Jose Reyes. With Reyes on first base in the fifth inning, Tampa Bay pitcher Chris Archer wanted to keep the speedy shortstop close to the base. He threw hard to the first baseman, but the ball hit Reyes as he was diving back to the base. There was an audible intake of air from every male member in the large crowd of 41,247 as they instinctively tried to jump back a row. To make matters worse, Reyes does not wear a protective cup. Would this make him second-guess that decision? "Not a chance," said Reyes. "I never wear a cup in my entire career so I don't want to start now. That was just an accident. Hopefully someone doesn't hit me there again because that was painful."

To add insult to injury, the Rays defeated the Jays to sweep the series and push the under-achieving Jays further out of playoff contention. "Two shots to the groin," said manager John Gibbons. "One to Reyes and one to this three-game series." The painful blow was a perfect metaphor for Blue Jays fans, who had such high expectations when the 2013 campaign began.

* * * *

"Jose Reyes is bursting with life and positive energy," Jerry Howarth described. "He is always happy and plays the game with a smile on his face—and boy, he can play. He has great leadership abilities and when Jose Bautista was hurt last year (2013) for the last two months, Reyes assumed that leadership role and did it well. It's no fluke that he's a four-time all star and I look forward to seeing him play a full season without injury."

J. P. RICCIARDI

In 2005, J. P. Ricciardi, then the Blue Jays GM, expressed his surprise at how few deals had been cut with the deadline fast approaching. "This is the latest I've ever seen nothing not happen," he said.

* * * *

After jettisoning $30 million in payroll and creating a hodge-podge of bargain basement talent and a few stars, Ricciardi referred to the mix as "a pot of stew." *Sports Illustrated* took him at his word. "In Toronto's kitchen, Ricciardi is baseball's frugal gourmet," they reported in their 2003 baseball preview issue.

ALEXIS RIOS

Alex Rios made his major league debut during the 2004 season and batted .286 in 111 games. In his sophomore season his average dipped to .262, but he showed a bit of pop in his bat with 14 homers. His promise seemed about to be ful-filled in 2006 as he led the American League in batting in the early going and had 11 homers and 43 RBI in 60 games. Based on his blazing start, Rios was selected to the AL All-Star team. Unfortunately, he was unable to play due to a staph infection in his leg. The injury sapped his strength and as a result his second-half stats faltered. His final numbers were 17 homers, 82 RBI, and a .302 average.

* * * *

Buoyed by a new one-year, two and a half million dollar contract and hopes of a larger deal to follow, Rios had another good year in 2007. Once again he made the All-Star team as a reserve, and this time he was healthy enough to compete in the State Farm Home Run Derby. He eventually lost to Vladimir Guerrero, but not before leading the pack with 19 homers in the preliminary rounds. He once again went into a post-All-Star Game funk, finishing the season with a .297 average, 24 HR, and 85 RBI. Largely based on his defensive play in right field, he nevertheless was named Blue Jays Player of the Year.

* * * *

Based on his obvious potential, Rios was signed to a 7-year, 70-million dollar contract in the spring of 2008. He responded by batting .291 with 15 homers, 79 RBI, and an impressive 32 stolen bases.

"He's very close to being a five-tool player with his speed, batting average, and power," Matt Stairs said. "He puts a lot of pressure on himself, and he is his own worst enemy. He settled down after he was traded from Toronto to Chicago and had a really good year in 2012. He's capable of putting up some monster numbers because he has some of the strongest hands I've ever seen. Once he gets in that happy-go-lucky stance where he finally figures it out, he'll continue to put up some big numbers."

* * * *

After playing 108 games in a Toronto uniform in 2009, Rios was an ex-Blue Jay. The writing was on the wall when he struck out five (5) times against the LA Angels of Anaheim in a June 4 matchup at Rogers Centre. This was no golden sombrero—this one was pure platinum and because the performance took place at home—in a 6-5 loss—it was the talk of the town. Rios was placed on waivers on August 7 and became a member of the White Sox organization.

* * * *

The move to the Windy City did not rejuvenate his bat, as he hit .199, a notch under the Mendoza Line, in his final 41 games. He did rebound in 2010, hitting 21 homers and batting a much more respectable .284. During the 2013 campaign, he was again placed on waivers and claimed by the Texas Rangers.

* * * *

In June 2009, Rios was forced to apologize for an incident involving a young autograph seeker and an abusive fan outside a gala for the Blue Jays' charity foundation, after it went viral on You Tube. Exiting the exclusive event wearing a tuxedo, Rios apparently refused to sign an autograph for the young fan. Provoked by taunts of "You're a bum," and "You should be happy anyone even wants your autograph," as well as references to his poor play and high salary, Rios shot back with a string of expletives. "It was a long day," explained Rios. "I couldn't help the team win and it was just bad. You expect fans to follow you, because they obviously like the way you play, they like what you do, so I don't think it's their fault. I just lost my cool in that situation, and it was bad."

Rios had struck out five times in the game against the Angels earlier that same day at Rogers Centre, bringing his consecutive whiff total to a team-record seven.

Manager Cito Gaston brought a touch of humor to Rios's strikeout run. When a reporter asked if the Angels had Rios's number, the skipper replied, "They'll call him on his cell—that's how much they had his number."

SCOTT ROLEN

"Scott Rolen was my locker partner," Matt Stairs said. "He was a guy that got to the ballpark and then hid. I don't know where he went! We always lost him. He was just a very intense guy, straightforward, didn't smile much. Almost didn't seem like he enjoyed the game, but that was his way of getting prepared—no nonsense, no messing around. Very serious all the time. Very good third baseman."

PHIL ROOF

Phil Roof is the correct answer to a pretty good trivia question. The question is: Who was the first player signed by the Toronto Blue Jays, two weeks prior to the 1976 MLB expansion draft?

The prototypical journeyman ballplayer, Roof was acquired from the Chicago White Sox for a player to be named later. He was a good defensive catcher with a strong arm to second, but his performance with the bat can only be called respectful; that is, he made little noise with it during games. Although he hung around the majors for 15 years, his career numbers don't so much shout as whisper—215 average, 43 homers, 210 RBI. His stay in Toronto was short. He took the field for the final time on May 30, 1977, and then retired after a 15-year career, at the age of 36.

B. J. RYAN

When a closer arrives with a bigger salary than Mariano Rivera, he'd better be good. Darn good. In November of 2005, B. J. Ryan inked a five-year, $47 million contract with the

Toronto Blue Jays. It was the largest amount ever shelled out for a major league reliever, the kind of deal that had baseball insiders abuzz, because it seemed to be a game-changer. Was this to be the new standard for closers, especially those who, like Ryan, had rather thin resumes? What started out as an exciting new chapter in Blue Jays history turned out to be a cautionary tale for team owners.

In the first year of Ryan's contract, the Jays had little reason to complain, as Ryan saved 38 games, third-best in the American League. And then came 2007.

Having his name linked to Rivera was a signal that he had arrived. Unfortunately, his name soon became linked to another famous pitcher—Tommy John. On May 11, 2007, the Jays announced that Ryan had undergone Tommy John Surgery on his left elbow and would be sidelined for the remainder of the season.

"B. J. Ryan had a tough year with us," Matt Stairs said. "He had a lot of injuries. He had definitely got overused when he was in Baltimore, and it hurt his arm. He was a veteran who accepted his role. If he wasn't going to be closing, he'd do whatever they asked of him."

Ryan returned with a bang a year later, on April 13 of 2008, recording a 10th-inning save. He finished the season with 32 saves, good for sixth place among AL closers. In 2009, his velocity dropped sharply and he was put on the 15-day DL early in the campaign. When he returned, he was demoted to middle reliever status and was released later in the year.

MARCO SCUTARO

"Marco Scutaro was a player you hated to play against, but once you got to know him on the same team, he was a great teammate. As an opponent, he'd always come up with a big hit. He'd always make that nice defensive play. He was a guy you'd look at and think he was having too much fun on the other team. He was just the type of guy you hated to face. Once you got on his team you just knew he was one of the funniest guys you ever played with. Boy, some of the sayings he would have! He was funny! He even made it funnier because he had the broken English," Matt Stairs said.

Need an example? "Hitting is so crazy," Scutaro once said. "You feel great today and get three hits. And the next day you show up and it's 'What happened to my mechanics? Where's my swing?' Sometimes I even Google it and the search comes up with no results."

BILL SINGER

While the first singer to perform for the Jays was Springhill, Nova Scotia's own Anne Murray, you could make a little extra pocket money with a well-placed trivia question about who the second was. The answer would be veteran right-hander Bill Singer, who was the Opening Day starter on April 7, 1977.

* * * *

Singer not only started the first regular season game the Jays ever played, but he also chucked the initial pitch in their first spring training outing against the NY Mets in Denedin, Florida. Lee

Mazzilli—later to play for the Jays—set a discordant note by driving his third delivery over the fence for a home run.

* * * *

A seasoned veteran, Singer had been a 20-game winner in both major leagues before coming to the Blue Jays. He went 20-12 with the National League LA Dodgers in 1969 and 20-14 with the California Angels of the American League in 1973.

SkyDome/Rogers Centre

When it opened, Toronto's SkyDome got as much media attention as the baseball team that was to play within its sparkling confines. The world of sport had never seen a structure quite like this before. For one thing, it cost approximately $500 million to build.

The SkyDome's official baseball christening came on June 5, 1989. A crowd of 48,378 fans filled every seat in the place and some that weren't even seats (they sold 79 tickets for seats that didn't exist). Most spent as much time looking around the imposing structure as they did following the action on the field. Of course, every hit, every double play, every error was inevitably declared "the first in SkyDome." Paul Molitor, of the visiting Milwaukee Brewers (later to call SkyDome home) got the first hit—a double—and later the first run. Fred McGriff struck the historic first home run in the second inning, but the Jays went on to lose the contest 5-3. Still, it's safe to say that no one went home disappointed after this one.

* * * *

When SkyDome first opened, most visiting players were spellbound by the new ballpark. However, there were rumblings of concern from Blue Jays players that it would not be as homer-friendly as their previous digs at Exhibition Stadium. When Bob Brenly was brought in to pinch hit in the first game there, he hit a long drive that many said would have been a homer in the previous home of the Jays. When asked about it after the game, a straight-faced Brenly said, "Well, I have never had any luck hitting in this park."

* * * *

In 1990, the gnats visited SkyDome. No, that's not some bizarre misspelling of Giants. This was not an interleague game with San Francisco. These were actual gnats. The structure was supposed to be the inanimate equivalent of a postman. Neither snow nor rain nor dark of night was supposed to get it from its appointed rounds. But no one mentioned gnats. The little creatures brought play to a standstill for more than half an hour as a swarm invaded the field of play. This was proof that even the almighty SkyDome had a few bugs to be worked out.

* * * *

In May of 2005, the National League's Washington Nationals made their first trip to Canada for a three-game Interleague series with the Blue Jays. The Nationals were, of course, previously known as the Expos and were Canada's first Major League entry. In 1997, a three-game series between Canada's two teams attracted an average of 40,681 fans. The series with Washington drew an average of 23,464, including a smattering of devoted 'Spos fans. A sad end after 36 years.

MATT STAIRS

Matt Stairs – Professional Hitter. It sounds more like a job resume than a nickname, the kind of thing you might see on a Mafioso's business card—or a throwback to Paladin's *Have Gun, Will Travel* greeting card. Except that with Stairs, it was "Have Bat, Will Travel."

You may recall that Paladin went where he was needed to sort out trouble, usually a showdown with the toughest guy in town. With a record 26 pinch hits, you could say the same about Matt.

Speaking of travel, Stairs did lots of that: Montreal, Japan, Boston, Oakland, Chicago (Cubs), Milwaukee, Pittsburgh, Kansas City, Texas, Detroit, Toronto, Philadelphia, San Diego, and Washington. With 13 Major League stops, he played for more teams than any position player in Major League history over the course of his 19-year career. He was a hired gun, brought in for one reason and one reason only—to hit.

Stairs was born in Saint John, New Brunswick, and attended Fredericton High School after his parents moved to the provincial capital.

* * * *

Like many Canadians, Stairs's first love is hockey. A knee injury prevented him from pursuing a rink career, although he had the talent to go far. He now coaches the Fredericton High School Black Cats in his New Brunswick hometown. "I wish I could have taken half of my 19 years in the big leagues and played 9 years in the NHL," he says. "It's in my DNA."

* * * *

He played two seasons with the Blue Jays in 2007 and 2008, and his lifetime average was .263, with a total of 265 homers while playing first base, the outfield, and serving time as a DH. Stairs was also a superb pinch hitter, surely one of the toughest hitting assignments of them all. He set the record for the most homers as a pinch hitter. He is only the second Canadian player to top the 35 home-run mark in a season.

In 2007, Stairs returned to his native country, signing a one-year minor league deal with the Blue Jays that included an invitation to spring training. He played himself onto the Major League roster and a spate of injuries presented him with ample playing time. The 39-year-old slugger responded to the opportunity, batting .289 for the year with 21 homers and 64 RBI.

Although better known for his long ball achievements, Stairs holds the record for the most consecutive doubles, establishing the mark on August 8, 2007.

Not surprisingly for a man with ice in his veins, Stairs was also a standout hockey player and still plays regularly in a Fredericton beer league. He also coaches the game at his high school alma mater.

At 29, Stairs was an old man by baseball standards by the time he became a legitimate major leaguer. Nevertheless, the New Brunswicker had longevity, sticking around the big leagues for 19 seasons.

Fellow Maritimer Hank Snow was famous for his song "I've Been Everywhere," but the country icon had nothing on Matt. After his debut with the Montreal Expos in 1992, he lived in more cities than *The Fugitive*, had more uniform changes than a mud-wrestling team, and sported more numbers than a University of Waterloo math exam. Fittingly, he ended his career as a member of the Washington Nationals, the new incarnation of Les Expos.

* * * *

Stairs described his first season with Toronto: "I was happy with my 2007 season. I worked on things and accepted my role of being a fourth outfielder and part-time guy, knowing I was going to get 300 at- bats. The biggest thing that year was that I wanted to change my stance to accommodate sitting on the bench for 5 or 6 days and then playing the next day. I had to learn to get in a good hitter's stance, an area I was going to be happy with. Mickey Brantley was my hitting coach, and we did a lot of work on that. We opened up to a wider stance with less movement, I think.

"I think that entire first month I didn't hit a home run and only had one RBI. Mickey kept telling me, 'Stay with it, it's going to work.' Because I was hitting balls in BP further than I ever had! And finally when I hit that first home run off of Reyes of Tampa Bay it just kind of went off from there and the home runs started coming, it seemed like every other day. Every other start, that is."

* * * *

On July 26, 2008, Stairs, with his stocky frame not exactly built for speed, legged out a triple against the Minnesota Twins.

"I remember because I hit the ball to left center," he recalls with a laugh. "I remember coming around second base saying *screw it, I'm going for it.* I think Brian Butterfield was the third base coach at the time and they were telling me to get down, and I slid and when I stood back up I was safe. I caught my spike on the bag and almost fell off the base," he said, laughing. "So I had my triple, I had them laughing in our dugout and then cheering and then laughing again because I almost fell off the bag. I got 13 of those [triples], and that's 13 more than a lot of people have."

* * * *

One of Stairs's most notable achievements was hitting five consecutive doubles. The 39-year-old completed the feat on August 8, 2007, making him the first Blue Jay to turn the trick. He was also the first major leaguer to do it in 14 seasons. Despite having only 400 at-bats, his season totals were impressive, as he batted .289 with 21 home runs and 64 RBI. "I don't think it was luck," he says. "I was swinging the bat well. Gibby [manager John Gibbons] moved me into the number-one spot in the order and left me at leadoff for eight or nine games. When you get in that groove, things just seem to click. There is some luck behind it because you still have to hit holes, but I knew I was seeing the ball well. I was taking pitches, waiting for my pitches to drive, and I can pretty much remember where all the pitches were and where the ball was hit too.

"They were pretty much all the same, either to right-center or down the left field line. It's hell battling pitchers sometimes. You think you're beaten and then the ball goes the opposite way and drops for a base hit. Two or three were against [Chien-Ming] Wang on the Yankees, and a couple against Baltimore. It is what it is, you get up there and getting a hit is pretty much lucky anyway because you've got to hit the right angle of the bat, you've gotta hit the ball right, and you've gotta hit it where someone's not standing. Hitting a round ball with a round bat is the toughest thing."

* * * *

Stairs holds the Major League record for most pinch-hit homers. "I think the number-one thing about being a pinch hitter is that you have to accept your role," he says modestly. While a member of the Philadelphia Phillies, his reputation as a pinch hitter continued to grow. T-shirts could be seen all over the ballpark recognizing his ability to come through in pressure-filled situations. One of the cleverest ones read: "In Case of Emergency, Use Stairs." Stairs loved the challenge of having the team's fortunes riding on him.

"I looked forward to it," he says. "I had a lot of confidence when managers asked me—'Stairs, you're hitting in the ninth inning second,' so I knew they had the confidence in me in that situation to go up and tie a game or try to win a game. I was never afraid to fail. If I struck out with the bases loaded in the ninth inning, it didn't bother me. I knew I might be back next day and have an opportunity to be a hero again, so I think that had a lot to do with it. I'm a pretty laid-back type of person and don't show a lot of emotion. I don't get fired up or too excited about things. But to own the Major League record, it's quite something, and to beat Mr. Cliff Johnson, it was quite an honor."

DAVE STEWART

Jays fans have bittersweet memories of Dave Stewart. On the sweet side, he is fondly remembered as a great, often overpowering pitcher for the '93 championship Jays squad. The bitter part came at the sight of the 6'2", 200-pound right-hander on the mound at SkyDome on June 29, 1990, throwing a no-hitter as a member of the visiting Oakland Athletics. Stewart was brilliant, pitching one of two Major League no-hitters that day. The second televised game featured the St. Louis Cardinals and LA Dodgers, and Fernando Valenzuela was the author of a no-no at Dodger Stadium. ESPN, which broadcast both games, had struck ratings gold with this no-hitting miniseries.

Three years later, Stewart had moved from the A's to the Jays and the sight of him on the mound was less upsetting and more uplifting to Blue Jay Nation. Featuring a fastball, slider, and forkball in his arsenal of pitches, Stewart was a towering, glowering presence.

* * * *

On the field, Stewart may have had a glare that would send young kids scampering for home, but off the field he was the most generous and warmhearted of men. In the midst of the

1993 ALCS with the Chicago White Sox, most players wanted to keep off-field distractions to a minimum. Not Stewart. While teammates spent Thanksgiving Day traveling to the Windy City to prepare for Game Six, he stayed behind and for several hours helped to serve turkey dinners to Toronto's homeless. And karma is a wonderful thing. The next night he took to the mound, glare and all, and was the winning pitcher in a 6-3 win over the White Sox as the Jays clinched the American League pennant.

But his good deeds didn't stop there. In Christmas of 1993, he hosted a party for 925 kids from the Boys and Girls Clubs of Canada. "Stew owns this town the way Robin Hood owned Sherwood Forest," said Jays president Paul Beeston.

Shannon Stewart

"Shannon Stewart, when he was in Minnesota, was in his prime and doing extremely well," Matt Stairs explained. "Unfortunately when he came over to Toronto, he wasn't healthy. He was hurt. He had a bad shoulder, which gave him a lot of trouble driving the barrel through the zone … Good guy, very supportive of knowing his role. He was going to be a fourth outfielder, starting out switching on and off with me, and we became good friends and rooted for each other."

* * * *

From his days playing high school baseball, and while a member of the Blue Jays, Stewart wore number 24. Why 24? "Ken Griffey Jr. and Rickey Henderson were my favorite players," he explained. "I could run like Rickey, and I wished I could hit homers like Griffey." When he was dealt to Minnesota in 2003, the number was already being worn by catcher Matt LeCroy. He started wearing # 23.

DAVE STIEB

D ave Stieb began his career as an outfielder, but he was always destined to be center stage, and where better to soak up the spotlight than the pitcher's mound. Of course they gave him a chance to make it as a position player. He batted under .200 in thirty-five games for Dunedin and posted a 2.08 in 26 innings on the mound. His future as a pitcher was pretty much sealed.

Once the Jays' brass convinced him of that, his ticket to the majors had been punched. Jays scout Bobby Mattick's appraisal said it all. "I like this boy's chances on the mound. He has a good arm. Will have a good slider. Do not care for him as an outfielder." A few years later, Mattick explained his thinking to Ron Fimrite. "Stieb knocked our eyeballs out," he said. "He was absolutely overpowering. We hadn't liked him as a hitter, but he sure as hell opened our eyes when he started pitching. We decided to draft him."

His first game as a Jay came in late June of 1979. Despite some period of adjustment, it was clear that he was a natural and needed very little work on his delivery or other mechanics. His release point, which some pitchers never quite find, seemed to come instinctively. His rookie season record of 8 wins and 8 losses might not seem impressive, but remember, this was a team that ran up 109 losses on the season, against only 57 wins. But not all his experience as a position player was wasted. He was among the best fielding pitchers in the game, thanks to his time in the outfield.

And there was something else. He could see pitching from a hitter's point of view. "Like Lemon," said then-Blue Jays pitching coach Al Widmar, "Dave knows how tough it is to hit. That gives him a psychological edge."

* * * *

Stieb was the lone Blue Jay selected to the American League All-Star team in 1980. It was only then that he realized just how little fans outside of Canada knew about his team. "We were a family team," he wrote in his autobiography (*Tomorrow I'll Be Perfect*). "Dave Who? Lloyd Who? Alfredo Who?"

* * * *

Stieb was the first Blue Jays starter to post a winning record for a complete season. He did it in the strike-shortened 1981 campaign, finishing with an 11-10 mark. He made the AL All-Star Game that year and even got a turn at bat thanks to a shortage of pinch hitters. Bruce Sutter struck him out.

* * * *

According to Dave Stieb, "the best move we made in '81 was to go on strike for forty-six games." At the time, the Jays' record was 16-42 which, according to one Toronto writer, put them on track for a 45-117 futility mark, "if we didn't go into a slump."

* * * *

In May of 1983, the Jays were playing the White Sox and slugger Ron Kittle hit a one-hopper back to the mound. The ball glanced off the glove of the usually sure-handed Stieb toward first baseman Willie Upshaw. Both men converged on the ball, but Stieb arrived first and kicked—yes kicked—the ball into Upshaw's outstretched glove. Stieb then proceeded on to cover first and Willie underhanded the ball to him to nip the runner. It was the one time that booting the ball actually *prevented* an error.

* * * *

Former Jays ace Dave Stieb was not a modest man, not in demeanor in talent. He had the swagger of a gunslinger who knew he had all the bullets. California Angels manager Gene Mauch once commented, "He's good, but I don't think there is anyone in the world as good as he thinks he is." When Stieb wrote his sports biography, the title reflected his usual understated opinion of himself: *Tomorrow I'll be Perfect*. Still, even experts like Ted Williams, who pursued hitting perfection, acknowledged his pitching gifts. "He's got a ton of talent," Ted once said. "For three or four years, he was as good as there was."

Stieb was always chasing perfection and on a few occasions, he almost overtook it. The pitcher had one no-hitter but came close to several others. In fact, in not one but two consecutive late-season starts in 1988, he had come within a single strike of the elusive landmark.

In 1989 he flirted with perfection on several more occasions. He had a good year, boasting a 17-8 record and a notable 3.35 ERA. He also added two more one-hitters to his resume, which gave him five for his career. He also pitched a game that fell one final out short of perfection. Twenty-six batters up, twenty-six batters down, and this was against the always-potent Yankees. Roberto Kelly ruined the perfect game by doubling on a 2-0 pitch. Steve Sax then added another hit.

Of the two 1989 one-hitters, the one against the Milwaukee Brewers was toughest to accept, at least by third baseman Kelly Gruber. Gruber made a diving knock-down play of a line drive but wasn't able to complete the throw in time to get the runner. The official scorer called it a hit. "That ball hit me in the mitt," said a disappointed Gruber. "It was a tough play, but I should have made it. It's tough to give a player an error when he dives for the ball, but I'm a firm believer that anytime a ball hits you in the mitt, you should make the play."

* * * *

"Even donkeys can shake their heads." This was former Toronto pitching coach Al Widmar's advice to pitchers who blame the catcher's pitch call. Stieb was often the target for this admonition.

* * * *

Discussing a particularly tough loss to Texas in August of 1985, Stieb concluded, "In every game there is a turning point and, for me in this one, it must have been the moment the ump said, 'Play ball!'"

* * * *

When things failed to go his way, Stieb had the well-earned reputation of placing the blame elsewhere, usually on his teammates. His stony stares at fielders who committed errors or just failed to make the play hardly endeared him to his teammates. Whenever an opposing player got a hit off him, he often looked amazed, as if to say "this can't be happening." In fairness, he did eventually mature and gave up the prima donna routine.

* * * *

Stieb also had a propensity for crotch-grabbing and may have been the most prolific in that department until Michael Jackson hit the stage to record *Thriller.*

* * * *

Every time Stieb took the mound, he looked like he'd walked out of Central Casting. Tall, handsome, and mustachioed, he was like a young Errol Flynn. Once on the mound, he seemed to be in a world of his own, talking to himself, fidgeting, looking around like a befuddled tourist on his first trip to the big city. At times, he also seemed in need of some anger management. The anger seldom seemed to be directed at himself, but rather at his supporting cast of fielders or at the catcher who had called for the pitch that had been hit. Or the opposing batter who had the gall to get a hit off him. After either event, he would place his hands on his hips and glare at the offending party with disdain. The infamous Stieb stink-eye. Or slap his glove repeatedly. Or the crotch-grab thing. At such times, it was as if he was the maestro and someone in the orchestra was caught playing a kazoo.

Former catcher and current Jays announcer Buck Martinez recalled such an event for *SI*. "He threw a home run pitch to Greg Luzinski in Chicago, and as the ball cleared the fence, Dave threw his hands up in the air and looked at me as if to say, 'How could you call that stupid pitch?' I had butted heads with him before about alienating his teammates, so we had a conversation the next morning about it." That conversation proved to be something of a turning point for the volatile pitcher. He apologized to Martinez and made a point of congratulating fielders for good plays instead of criticizing them for bad ones.

"He thanked me for my apology," recalled Stieb. "No way he should be thanking me. That showed me something, made me feel even worse, and I already felt pretty bad about the whole thing. I'm a real competitor who just doesn't deal too well with failure. I realize now I could've had my butt kicked for the stuff I used to do. I was fortunate to have players around me who could deal with all that. Remember, I'd been an outfielder most of my life, so I'd never had to deal with anyone making an error behind me. All I had to worry about was myself. I said a lot of things I shouldn't have. I realize now how bad all that looked."

* * * *

Stieb and the Blue Jays management seemed to always be at odds. Invariably those disputes involved his demands to be traded. Finally details for a long-term contract were worked out and peace was restored. But naturally, Blue Jays fans, and Torontonians in general, took it personally. Stieb went on an off-season good will tour of the city to mend fences. Trent Frayne of the *Toronto Sun* expressed the feelings of many fans. "Stieb often leaves the impression that pitching in Toronto is like playing for the Bangkok Beavers."

* * * *

Many years later, Stieb shook his head at the ease with which he made the transition from the outfield to the mound. "It boggles me now, especially after what I've been through, that ability I had to throw the slider. I could just push a button and here comes a slider on the black."

In truth, Stieb's parents, Pete and Pat, should be given much of the credit for his pitching success. They had forbidden him to pitch in youth baseball. No, he wasn't forced to practice the violin instead; in fact, they were very supportive of his baseball pursuits. They just wanted to protect his arm from injury. Stieb's high school coach failed to convince him to take the mound. Despite the urging of a pro scout, so did John Oldham, his coach with the San Jose City College Salukis. "Maybe," Oldham told *SI*, "the outfield saved his arm."

Stieb finally relented and threw some batting practice pitches. Pitching coach Mark Newman told coach Oldham that Stieb had a better curveball than any of the pitchers in the rotation. The real miracle is that, although Stieb ended up pitching only 17 ½ innings for the Salukis, scout Mattick saw two of them. The rest is Blue Jays history.

It was a life-changing moment for the young ballplayer. Being told that something was bad for you and then being told it was your future. "It was hard for me to fathom why they wanted me to be something I wasn't," Stieb said. "I don't think I even knew how to figure an ERA in those days."

TODD STOTTLEMYRE

Todd Stottlemyre might not have been the best pitcher the Blue Jays ever sent to the mound, but he was surely one of the most temperamental. The son of former New York Yankee great Mel Stottlemyre, he featured a 95-mile-an-hour fastball and a challenging style. The rest of his arsenal consisted of a very decent slider, an above average curveball, and later in his career, a split-finger fastball. There was very little subtlety about him, no changeup to set up his fastball, no patience for nibbling at the corners of the plate.

Nevertheless, Todd was an integral part of the Blue Jays' back-to-back World Series championships in '92 and '93. In Game Four of the '93 Series, he was involved in a less-than-graceful play at third. Attempting to slide head-first into the base after a Roberto Alomar single, he was an easy out. Apparently, Philadelphia mayor Ed Rendell found Stottlemyre's base running efforts humorous and shared these feelings with reporters. He also announced that even he could get a hit off the Blue Jay pitcher. Of course the good mayor had to eat some crow when the Blue Jays prevailed and won their second-straight World Series. As the Jays celebrated their championship, Stottlemyre paused long enough to invite the City of Brotherly Love's head honcho to "Kiss my **s!"

MIKE TIMLIN

"Not many players can wear four World Series rings at the same time, but Mike can. Two with the Blue Jays and two with the Red Sox. His niche was the eighth inning, and he was as good as any in that role," Jerry Howarth said. "He was able to get the last out in the '92 World Series, so he showed his versatility and ability to perform under fire. He was a wonderful family man with those young kids of his. He and his wife are just tremendous people. Mike stands for so much above the game and outside the game as a person, a pillar in the community, someone who maximized his ability, and then some. He pitched for close to 20 years [17 seasons]."

TOM UNDERWOOD

Some players just don't seem to get much run support. It's tough to explain, but that's just the way it is. They are known as "hard-luck pitchers." In 1978 and 1979, Tom Underwood fit that description. It wasn't that he hadn't pitched well, despite his 3-7 record. If only those Blue Jays bats would come alive when he was on the mound …

On June 26, the Jays were playing at home against the Baltimore Orioles. Future Blue Jay Mike Flanagan was on the mound for the O's and Underwood expected another night when runs would be as scarce as a hen's teeth. He needn't have worried. Baltimore scored a run in the first, but this wasn't destined to be a nail-biter. The Jays exploded for 24 runs and won the game 24-10, presenting Underwood with a rare laugher.

WILLIE UPSHAW

"Willie is a tremendous person and family man," Jerry Howarth said. "He was part of the litany of great first basemen in Blue Jays history, which is saying something because the Jays have been blessed at that position. Willie is from a big family and his mom and dad were very caring people. We'd go to Arlington, Texas, to play the Rangers and the hotel swimming pool would be filled with Upshaws. It was fun to watch."

* * * *

It wasn't the finest hour in Blue Jays history. In fact, it was the inning from hell, a manager's nightmare. On August 24, 1983, in the top of the tenth inning of a game against the Baltimore Orioles in Baltimore, things were looking good for the Jays. Anytime you can win an extra-inning game on the road is a good day.

With Barry Bonnell on first, the Jays already held a 4-3 lead and there were no outs. Bonnell possessed decent speed, and manager Bobby Cox gave the steal sign. Bonnell took a cautious lead and then expanded it. Orioles pitcher Tippy Martinez picked him off. One out.

Still no reason to panic. The lead was intact. Dave Collins came to the plate and drew a walk. He too was picked off.

Willie Upshaw ambled to the plate and beat out an infield hit. Lo and behold, he was picked off too.

The Orioles had gotten out of the inning without Martinez retiring a single batter.

Buoyed by the three pick-offs, the Orioles rallied to tie the score in the bottom of the 10th frame. With two men aboard, Sakata then hit a home run to win the game by a 7-4 margin.

If there is a moral to this story, it might be … ah heck, there is no moral to this story.

* * * *

Willie Upshaw was the first Blue Jay player to drive in 100 runs, finishing with 104 RBI in 1983.

* * * *

As a rookie, New Brunswick's Paul Hodgson sometimes roomed with Upshaw on road trips. "He always made sure I was looked after," recalls the former Blue Jay. "We called him Hard Will because he had 2 percent body fat and was as strong as you can imagine. He was a cousin of NFL player Gene Upshaw."

TOM VERDUCCI

D on't remember the name? Before you go scrambling for the *Baseball Register*, there's a reason for that. Verducci is a talented writer for *Sports Illustrated* and in February of 2005 he got an assignment that many of us would, if not kill, at least maim for. He would be spending five days as a member of the Toronto Blue Jays and would then write about the experience. The result of his investigative reporting was a cover story in the March 14, 2005, issue of *SI*, entitled "I was a Toronto Blue Jay." Pictured with him on the cover were Reed Johnson, Vernon Wells, and Frank Catalanotto. The fact that the five days were during spring training and therefore won't appear in any Major League record books doesn't really matter.

Verducci was at the plate during some indoor pitching practice with 6'6", 225-pound Roy Halladay on the mound. "Halladay's fastball is angry," wrote Verducci, "announcing its indignation with an audible hum that grows frighteningly loud as it approaches. His slider is even more evil because it presents itself in the clothing of a fastball, but then, like a ball rolling down the street and falling into an open manhole, drops out of sight, down and away. His curveball bends more than an election-year politician."

The next pitcher to warm up is Miguel Batista and hitters Vernon Wells, Reed Johnson, and Frank Catalanotto politely insist that Verducci go first. Only later did he discover that Batista had hit three Jays players in the head during the previous year's spring training. "So I am the royal taster," suggested Verducci. "The three outfielders want me in there to gauge Batista's control … He throws me one pitch that I swear breaks two ways—first left, then right—like a double-breaker putt in golf—only at about 900 mph."

CHIEN-MING WANG

Chien-Ming was only the fourth major leaguer to hail from Taiwan. He debuted with the New York Yankees in 2005 and remained in pinstripes until 2009. The finesse pitcher features an excellent sinker, an above-average slider, and a fastball that can reach the mid-nineties. He subsequently played in Washington for the Nationals and in June of 2013 became a Toronto Blue Jay.

Back in 2008, when Wang was a Yankee and Vernon Wells was still a member of the Blue Jays, the center fielder had this to say about the Taiwanese right-hander. "The difference between [Wang] and other sinkerballers is that [the ball] moves so late. Because he throws it so hard, you don't have time to react. You commit to it, but by the time you start your swing, the ball is almost in the dirt. You know what's coming, but it just doesn't matter."

DUANE WARD

"Ward was a fierce competitor. You didn't want to be around him during those years as an opponent because he would take that hard curveball and just strike you out and have fun doing it. The Jays definitely would not have won '92 and '93 World Series rings without him. He was really one of the most valuable players they had among so many great ones. He was the set-up man in the eighth inning for Henke in '92 and the closer in '93," Howarth said. "For me, when he had to have shoulder surgery after the '93 season stands out to this day as the most significant injury the Blue Jays have ever had, because they have not gone back to the playoffs since."

MITCH WEBSTER

When outfielder Mitch Webster was dealt to the Chicago Cubs after first playing in Montreal for the Expos and then for the Blue Jays, he looked on the bright side. "It'll be great not to have to listen to two national anthems," he said.

DAVID WELLS

David Wells was larger than life in more ways than one. Physically, he was a cross between his hero (Babe Ruth), Rob Ford, and Fat Elvis. Famous for wearing a Babe Ruth t-shirt under his uniform, he was infamous for the level of his … insubordination. Wells could be brilliant or he could be seemingly blasé.

Perhaps it was a side effect of being a relief pitcher, but David Wells had the habit of walking in his sleep while a member of the Blue Jays. On one nocturnal amble in 1987, he shattered a window and lacerated the thumb of his pitching hand. Not long after that, he fell down while sleepwalking. Wells was philosophical about the incidents. "I'm not going to lose any sleep over it," he said.

Around the same time that Wells was experiencing these bouts of somnambulism, fellow Jays pitcher Mike Flanagan slipped in the bathroom, injuring his eye when it struck the shower door. His explanation, when it finally came, was worth the wait. "It took me awhile, but I finally figured out how it happened," he said. "David Wells was sleepwalking and pushed me through the door."

* * * *

In Wells's second arrival in Toronto, after being traded from the Yankees in one the most spectacular swaps in recent baseball history (Homer Bush, Graeme Lloyd, and Wells for Roger Clemens), he made it onto the July 10, 2000, cover of *Sports Illustrated*, although the accompanying article was less than flattering, at least as far as his physique is concerned.

Dispelling the notion that Wells is a fat guy in search of a skinny body, writer Jeff Pearlman disagreed. "Wells is a fat guy who is content being fat, and if he is in search of anything, it is a beer."

Pearlman also noted Wells's famous aversion to physical fitness and spring training preparation. "Wells, who routinely reports to camp disguised as a weather balloon, views it as vital wiener roasting time." And this was a *positive* piece on Boomer.

* * * *

Managers love pitchers who want the ball in key situations. A pitcher who happily, willingly gives up the ball when he is yanked by the manager is no competitor. However, even that time-honored baseball maxim has its limits. Limits that David Wells apparently doesn't recognize.

In an August 1991 home game against the Boston Red Sox, Jays manager Cito Gaston went to the mound to get Wells after the pitcher had given up nine hits and five runs. When he put out his hand to get the ball, as is the custom, Wells refused to give it up. The two had words and Boomer threw a mini tantrum, throwing the ball down the left field line, much to the displeasure of his manager. The final score was 12-7 for the Red Sox.

* * * *

On June 5, 1988, the Blue Jays ran roughshod over the Boston Red Sox at Fenway Park. The final score was 12-4 for the Jays. While the win was decisive, the identity of the winning pitcher was not. The decision was in the hands of official scorer Chaz Scoggins, veteran writer for the *Lowell Sun*. Invoking rule 10.19 (c), Scoggins made the determination that the "W" should go to reliever Duane Ward. The rule gives the scorer responsibility of choosing the pitcher deemed "most effective."

The following day, the writer got a phone call from Greg Clifton, the agent for Jays reliever David Wells. Wells had pitched 2 innings, in which he struck out two, walked one, and allowed 3 hits. He was replaced by Ward, who also pitched 2 scoreless innings with a hit and a walk. Clifton tried to have the decision changed so that his client would get credit for the win. He cited the fact that several outraged fans had called the Red Sox to complain about the injustice. Closer investigation showed that almost all of the callers had Wells in their Rotisseries League.

* * * *

David Wells could be critical of other ballparks, as indicated by his commentary while watching *When It Was a Game,* a baseball documentary. When spidery black and white footage of Tiger Stadium from 1934 was shown, he became especially animated. "There's Tiger Stadium. Look, same small dugouts. Look, same clubhouse. Hey… same postgame spread!"

VERNON WELLS

"Vernon was a Gold Glover here for three straight years and had this huge year in 2003 when he led the Blue Jays in total hits with 215—still the Blue Jays record," Howarth explained. "He is a very fine person, wonderful father and husband and someone who certainly got the most out of his career. In addition he was able to also fight through the adversity of not having good years and being booed at home. He did not let that affect him even though it hurt him off the field when he would go home and have that to live with. I always admired how he handled that negativity around him when he wasn't doing well. Vernon always gave his very best."

* * * *

In their May 15, 2006, edition, *Sports Illustrated* ran one of their Pop Culture Grids surveys, and Vernon Wells was one of the featured athletes. The survey gave us such invaluable insights as his shoe size ("12"), who people tell him he resembles ("Daunte Culpepper"), the last book he had read ("the Bible"), whether he had tried yoga ("No. Too much concentration"), the thing that drives him crazy ("dog hair on my sheets and pillows"), and— most embarrassing of all—his favorite love song ("Because You Loved Me," by Celine Dion).

* * * *

When Eric Hinske won the Rookie-of-the-Year award in 2002, Vernon Wells was ineligible because he had accumulated more than the maximum allowable 130 career at-bats during September call-ups from 1999-2001. His first full year was nonetheless impressive for the lack of hardware. He hit 23 homers, scored 87 runs, batted a solid .275, and had 100 RBI. He was also a defensive standout.

After the Blue Jays failed to make the playoffs in 2006, Vernon Wells was hired as a postseason analyst for ESPN's *Baseball Tonight*. The reviews were generally good, but not those from teammates. "I got plenty of calls from friends and team-mates that were not as nice," he admitted. "A former teammate of mine, Eric Hinske, sent me a text message that said, '*Your nose looks even bigger on TV*'."

* * * *

It may not be a milestone that he especially cherishes, or even recalls, but in his final year as a Jay, Wells stroked a two-run homer that put Philadelphia Phillies pitcher Jamie Moyer in the record books. The round-tripper was the 506th allowed by Moyer, making him Major League Baseball's all-time leader in that category.

* * * *

Wells is in the Hall of Fame. No, not the one in Cooperstown, NY. He's in the Baseball Humanitarians Hall of Fame which, depending on how you look at it, might be even better. He was inducted in 2010 following his selection as the Branch Rickey Award winner for his humanitarian works. Dave Winfield had previously won the award in 1992 while a member of the Blue Jays.

DEVON WHITE

"He hailed from Kingston, Jamaica," Howarth said of White. "I knew the family. He was a wonderful athlete, beautiful person, great father and as graceful a center fielder as you'd ever want to find. He hardly ever left his feet because he could glide to the ball going at full speed and made tough plays look easy."

It was December of 1990, and baseball's winter meetings were in full swing. The California Angels were looking for a second baseman, specifically Steve Sax of the New York Yankees. Unable to reach a deal with the pinstripers, they looked farther north—to Toronto—and obtained Luis Sojo in a six-player deal that also included center fielder Devon White. White was known as a talented defensive player, but the Angels had deemed him a bust with the bat. The Yankees obviously agreed. And you can hardly blame them. In 1989 White was so impotent at the plate that the halos sent him to the minors, basically for a remedial class in hitting. The 27-year-old finished the season with the parent club but received the equivalent of a failing grade, with a .217 season average. It wasn't hard to read between the lines in Angel GM Mike Port's farewell to White: "Toronto is getting a man of supreme physical ability. Maybe we just didn't find the right key."

Even Jays GM Pat Gillick avoided the subject of hitting when he commented to the press. While allowing that White's speed might combine with the SkyDome's artificial turf to help his offense, he mostly played up his obvious strength. "We're looking to Devon White for defense," he admitted.

* * * *

It was the first deal ever consummated between the two franchises, and one of the best the Jays ever swung. And all because the Yankees wanted to keep Steve Sax. In Toronto, White's bat came to life. In his five years as a Jay, he batted a respectable .270 with 72 home runs, including two 17-homer seasons.

* * * *

Devon was one of those rare outfielders who was so good that he made it look easy. They say that Joe DiMaggio was like that. He seemed to glide, rather than run, and made even spectacular plays look routine.

In Toronto, they call it The Catch. In the rest of the baseball world, that capitalized caption belongs under a grainy black and white photo of Willie Mays. And baseball is a game of tradition and lore. You don't step on Superman's cape, you don't spit into the wind, you don't pull the mask off the old Lone Ranger, and you sure as heck don't mess around with the "greatest catch ever made."

Willie Mays's catch of a drive off the bat of Vic Wertz is etched in baseball history as the most effective use of leather since the cavemen discovered they could wear the stuff. The over-the-shoulder catch in Game One of the 1954 World Series remains one of baseball's iconic moments. As always, World Series hits, catches, steals, and other on-field performances are magnified tenfold. Mays pursued the ball with the focus of a heat-seeking missile, his cap flying off in the process. And Mays's catch was followed by a spin that would have made Serge Savard proud. And then there was the throw. It was all done as if choreographed, then shot in black and white to be the essential defensive play of all time—the definition of defense. The game was tied at the time and there were no outs in the eighth inning, with two men aboard.

And yet a very strong case can be made for Devon White's grab being better.

Given the stage and the drama, it was certainly the best defensive play in Blue Jays history. The stage was Game Three of the 1992 World Series between the Jays and the National League champion Atlanta Braves. To set the scene, there were runners on first and second, no one out, and the always-dangerous David Justice at the plate for the Braves. Justice laid into a Juan Guzman fastball and launched a long drive toward the center-field fence. At first it looked like it might be a home run. Using his tremendous speed, the divine Devon set off in hot pursuit and arrived at the wall just in time to leap and use his full extension to make the catch, almost embedding himself in the wall in the process.

He then wheeled and threw the ball on a line to cutoff man Roberto Alomar. Alomar relayed the ball to John Olerud at first in an attempt to double-up the runner, although the throw was unnecessary since Terry Pendleton had been called out for running past lead runner Deion Sanders. Olerud threw across the diamond to Kelly Gruber at third and Gruber set off in pursuit of Deion, who was retreating to second base. Video later showed that Gruber managed to tag him out with a desperate diving lunge; however, the umpire missed the call and the Jays were robbed of a spectacular triple play. For starters, White saved two runs from scoring.

Many observers, including iconic announcer Vin Scully, compared it with Mays's legendary catch. Scully is one of the few people who could say, with ample verification, that they had seen both up close and personal. It is practically heresy to suggest that anything could be more sublime than the Mays catch. Willie's came in an all-New York rivalry and in the media center of the baseball world. "I saw both catches," said the authoritative voice of the Dodgers. "And this one, to me, was better." He went on to explain that the looming presence of the wall made it a more difficult challenge for Devon.

"The big thing with Mays was that he had a wide-open area," Scully told Jayson Stark, a writer for *ESPN.com*. "He didn't have to be concerned with the wall. And that's a major concern. So I'm inclined to think that White's catch might have been better than Mays'."

Perhaps Dave Winfield's observation was best. And most diplomatic.

"We used to have to watch it in black and white," Winfield said of the Mays catch. "Now we can watch it in color."

As for White, he wisely avoided the comparisons. Willie Mays was a once-in-a-lifetime ballplayer, and The Catch was just one part of his body of work. For White, it has become the cornerstone of his career.

"What I did, that's just part of my game. I made that play, but I just thought of it as another play. It saved the game. And of course, it was the World Series, so it was a very important play in the game. But I would never compare myself with Willie Mays."

You don't mess with baseball tradition.

* * * *

White was a superb fielder, but even he missed one once in a while. After being booed for dropping a fly ball as a member of the Florida Marlins, he said, "I look up in the stands and I see them miss some too."

* * * *

Devon White was never one to phone it in. Okay, maybe once. During a game between the Milwaukee Brewers and California Angels in Anaheim on June 25, 1988, Devon White, then a member of the Angels, was on the phone in the clubhouse. The only problem with that is that the game had started and the Angels only had two outfielders. With the count 0-1 on Brewers leadoff man Jim Gantner, the game had to be restarted with the sheepish White back in the field.

ERNIE WHITT

"Ernie was from nearby Detroit so it was almost like he was part of Toronto. He became part of the fabric of Canada, using his baseball background to promote and grow the game. He's meant a lot to this country in his post-Blue Jays career," Jerry Howarth said.

* * * *

In the early to mid-eighties, Ernie shared catching duties with Buck Martinez, giving the Blue Jays amazing strength behind the plate. Whitt excelled defensively and offensively during those years. "That's when they formed one of the great platoon tandems in Blue Jays history," recalls Howarth.

Howarth elaborated on the particular difficulties of the catching position: "Catchers have to do their homework across the board in order to handle a staff of thirteen or more over the course of a season. They have to be able to appreciate their opponents and when the hitter steps in the box know what the hitter's weakness is and how to exploit it. At the same time they have to try to hit too and drive in some runs. There's a lot involved. It's probably the most demanding position easily in the game—and why so many become both managers and broadcasters and very skilled, insightful broadcasters. Ernie was one of the very best."

* * * *

On October 5, 1985, the Blue Jays were leading the Yankees by a tenuous 2-game margin with just two left to play in the season. Playing the Yankees at home, the Jays were in charge of their own fate. A win would bring the franchise their first-ever division title. Ernie Whitt started the hit parade for Toronto, homering in the second inning to stake the Jays to a 1-0 lead. They went on to win 5-1, as Lloyd Moseby and Willie Upshaw also went deep.

* * * *

It was September 14, 1987, the day it rained homers. The Toronto Blue Jays were home to the Baltimore Orioles at old Exhibition Stadium. Ernie Whitt homered into the right-field bleachers in the bottom of the 2nd. He hit another in the 5th and then powered a 3rd in the seventh. The ecstatic hometown fans cheered him during his final home run trot around the bases, and demanded that he emerge from the dugout to take a bow. The affable catcher complied, doffing his cap and waving to the crowd.

Rance Mulliniks hit two more dingers on that day, and George Bell added two of his own. Lloyd Moseby contributed another and Rob Ducey yet another. Fred McGriff completed the amazing show of power with the last four-bagger of the day. When the dust had settled and the score had been tallied, the scoreboard showed an 18-3 Blue Jay win—and an amazing

10 homers for the Jays. The Orioles' rookie center fielder chipped in with one for the O's.

* * * *

Whitt was a catcher who liked to talk. In fact, a magazine once rated him the most talkative catcher in the American League. It wasn't so much that he is a social person, although he decidedly is; it was more to distract the hitters from their task. Sometimes it worked, other times, not. He once engaged future Hall of Famer George Brett in conversation in hopes that the great hitter would lose his concentration. Knowing that Brett liked golf, Whitt once asked him about his game and how it was progressing. Brett dug into the batting box and started describing the smallest details of his golf game. Even as the pitcher wound up and delivered the pitch, he kept talking. "I'm swinging the club well," he said. "I shot an 84 on this really tough course …" Further details had to be put on hold, as Brett swung at the pitch and lined the ball off the outfield fence. The next thing Whitt knew, Brett was staring at him from second base. Next time up the subject was fishing and Brett again elaborated on his pursuits in that gentle sport. Again the pitch arrived mid-sentence but this time, Brett popped out. Third time up, he stepped into the batter's box, turned to Whitt, and said, "Let's go back to golf."

* * * *

Although he could never be called fat, Ernie Whitt liked his donuts. During a 1985 game in Oakland, the amiable catcher tried to bunt his way on base and was thrown out by a considerable margin. He returned to the dugout and was catching his breath while the on-deck batter was loosening up, swinging the weighted bat. When he had completed his regimen, he removed the batting donut which rolled in front of the dugout. Manager Bobby Cox couldn't resist. "Quick, someone get that before Ernie eats it," he said.

Like Whitt with donuts, his teammates couldn't stop at just one jibe. Next inning, when the Jays returned to the dugout, Whitt discovered that his batting helmet had been tampered with. "Someone had fixed a wire from the top of my batting helmet," he said later. "A donut hung from one end in front of the helmet, like a carrot for a donkey."

Even years later, Whitt still suspected the prankster was relief pitcher Bill Caudill, although Jim Clancy was another likely suspect. A few days earlier, Whitt had dumped a bucket of cold water over the washroom partition and onto the head of the preoccupied Clancy. Clancy responded by cutting one of Whitt's pant legs off.

* * * *

Ernie Whitt was fighting for the catcher's job at spring training in 1979. Competition with fellow catching candidates Rick Cerone and Bob Davis was intense. Near the end of camp, the Jays played a game with the National League's St. Louis Cardinals. After the game, Whitt was ecstatic and hopeful that he had impressed the right people. He had thrown out three of four of the Cardinals' speedy base runners and chipped in with a pair of timely hits. When he was called to Roy Hartsfield's office, however, the manager said, "I personally don't think you're able to catch at the big league level. You have a difficult time throwing people out." Hartsfield concluded that Whitt would be sent to the minors for another year of seasoning.

Whitt was shocked. "Did you not see me throw out three of the four base runners?" he asked.

"I saw that," Hartsfield conceded, "but they were slow runners."

"Excuse me?" said a stunned Whitt. "Lou Brock is a slow base runner?"

Hartsfield's back was now up. "That's my opinion and I'm sticking with it," he said. "I just don't think you can catch at the big league level and you'll definintely never catch in the big leagues for me."

"Well, Roy," replied Whitt, "I don't think you can manage at the big league level. You don't know talent."

By August 19, the Jays were out of contention. The final record was a dismal 53-109. Meanwhile, Whitt had captured the Silver Glove Award as the best defensive catcher in the minor leagues.

* * * *

One classic Ernie Whitt story relates to superstition and gamesmanship. Hall of Fame third baseman Wade Boggs was one of the most superstitious ballplayers to ever play the game. Many of his superstitions revolved around the number 7. In 1984 contract talks with the Boston Red Sox, he asked for a salary of $717,000. Before 7:30 night games, he insisted on running onto the field at precisely 7:17. If it was a day game with a 1:30 start, he crossed the white lines at 1:17, and so on. Desperate to do anything to disrupt the routine of the all-time great, Jays manager Bobby Cox conspired with the scoreboard operator at old Exhibition Stadium to stop the clock at 7:16 and restart it at 7:18. While the rest of the visiting Red Sox field took the field, Boggs could still be seen staring from the dugout, unsure of what to do.

When he finally came to bat, he turned to Whitt, who he believed for some reason to be the guilty party. "You're ****ing with me Whitt! I can't believe you're doing this to me." Boggs proceeded to go 0-4 in the game.

* * * *

Every fan knows that catching is a tough job, but we really don't know the half of it. Not only do they have to worry about calling pitches, trapping throws in the dirt, and enduring foul tips in the face, but they often have to battle the umps too. Whitt had a great relationship with umpire Kenny Kaiser, one of the most respected arbiters in the game. In his book *Catch*, he described what went on: "A lot of times I'll walk up to him and hit him right in the cup, just to set the tone for the day, and he'll say 'Oh, you %$%$^%, I'll get you.' And sure enough, I've walked away from games with bruises on my ribs where he's rabbit-punched me or closed his knees up hard into my sides. Quite often, I'll get down in my position and he'll have his foot sticking up so that I'll sit right down on his toe. We had a great time."

* * * *

When Whitt first faced fastballer Nolan Ryan, Kenny Kaiser was home plate umpire. The first pitch hit the catcher's mitt with a loud *thwaack*. "Strike one," yelled Kaiser, raising his right hand. Whitt turned to address the umpire. "Kenny, I didn't even see that ball and I know damn well you didn't see that ball."

"It sounded like a strike," explained Kaiser.

* * * *

Whitt confesses that the area occupied by catcher and ump can be very confining, not to say intimate. "I've had to tell a few of these guys to back off, that I'm already happily married," he once said.

* * * *

The last thing a manager wants to hear when he calls the bullpen for assistance is "Sorry, he can't come to the phone." If it had been left up to Ernie Whitt in a 1980 game against the Cleveland Indians, that might well have been the case. Whitt was upset at being left out of the starting lineup that day and when the phone rang, he knew it was manager Bobby Mattick bringing him in to pinch-hit. It was the ninth inning with two out. "Don't answer it," Whitt recalls telling bullpen coach John Felske. "I don't want to hit." Eventually, of course, he gave in and went to the plate. And the at-bat brought him a measure of fame, or perhaps infamy. He became the final out of a perfect game thrown by Indians ace Len Barker.

* * * *

Paul Hodgson remembers Ernie Whitt as a friendly man who helped a young rookie feel more at home. "He was a good friend while we were teammates. Obviously he was a great leader with a strong work ethic. He put his head down and played hard every day. He was one of the guys who made it much easier for a 20-year-old to come up to the big leagues and feel welcome. He treated me as if I was a guy who had ten years in. He helped make life livable for a young guy from New Brunswick.

"For all intents and purposes, Ernie is an honorary Canadian. He coaches the national team and works with Baseball Canada. He's an ambassador for baseball in this country."

JIMY WILLIAMS

Outfielder George Bell was not a fan of then-third base coach Jimy Williams. In his book, *Hardball*, he described an incident in Game Two of the 1985 playoff series against the Kansas City Royals. During the game, both Bell and Tony Fernandez had ignored Williams's signs to stop, and had scored runs. Bell claimed that Williams had given the sign too late. When Williams was asked about the two players, he told reporters, "Guess I'll have to get some Dominican stop signs." Bell did not see the humor.

* * * *

On the other hand, Ted Williams, the former Boston Red Sox great, was a fan of his namesake. "I like the little [Jimy] Williams guy. I like the way he yanks the pitchers. If they're not performing, he doesn't fool around—he yanks 'em out. Only way to do it, *only way*! I think he's doing a good job. He's making the tough decisions and doing it the way he thinks he should. You can't criticize that."

Not surprisingly, Ted had the same reputation for removing pitchers quickly when he managed the Washington Senators/Texas Rangers in the early 1970s.

* * * *

Williams was once asked to explain where his hometown of Arroyo Grande, California, was located, exactly. "It's three miles past Resume Speed," he replied.

Dave Winfield

"[Dave]was the first player—and still is the only player—to get a Toronto fan base that's relatively conservative and not really anticipatory of what's happening in the game, *into the game*! He made them vocal, got the fans up and into the games in 1992—to the point where it's never been exceeded. Dave made that possible. Dave Winfield is as nice a professional as it gets. He played into his early forties and is just a tremendous character guy. He was drafted in three sports (baseball, basketball, football), which just shows you what an athlete he is," Howarth said.

* * * *

It was only one year in a 22-year Hall of Fame career, but Blue Jays fans will take it. Dave Winfield came to the Blue Jays in 1992 from the California Angels. But Jays fans already knew him well, in fact intimately, on a first name—and sometimes other names—basis. The Angels were interested in re-signing him and Seattle and Boston were also interested in acquiring his services, but the outspoken outfielder declared that Toronto is "the only team that's not messed up."

* * * *

You've heard about ballplayers who have spent only a short time in the majors. In baseball parlance, such a short stint in the big leagues is called "a cup of coffee." In 1994, baseball was in a strike situation. While it was under way, Winfield was traded from the Minnesota Twins to the Cleveland Indians for "a player to be named later." When negotiations failed, the season was canceled. The 1994 season had been halted two weeks earlier (it was eventually canceled a month later on September 14 and Winfield never did suit up as a Cleveland Indian). The "player to be named later" was never named. Instead front office personnel from Cleveland were invited to dinner by their Minnesota counterparts. It is the only time a player has been traded for a dinner. Perhaps to avoid embarrassment, the deal was officially registered as a sale.

* * * *

Despite his Hall of Fame career, some critics would doubtless have labelled Winfield a baseball failure if not for what he later called "one stinkin' little hit." George Steinbrenner had famously referred to him as Mr. May (in contrast to another villified Steinbrenner employee named Reggie Jackson, a.k.a. Mr. October). The Boss was referring to the fact that Winfield had gone 1-for-22 (.045 average) in the 1981 World Series between the Yanks and eventual champion LA Dodgers. More than a decade later, the hurtful label was still firmly attached to Winfield. One writer for the *Washington Post* said earlier in the 1992 season that Winfield "may be the first player in baseball history to get 3,000 hits, none of them important." That one odorous little hit changed all that.

* * * *

The odorific hit that he refers to was a strike with two out, in the 11th inning of the pressure cooker that was the 1992 October Classic. It was a two-run double and was his first extra-base knock in 44 World Series at-bats. But if you think this two-bagger was needed to ensure Winfield a place in the Hall of Fame, think again. Blue Jays teammate Jack Morris scoffed at the idea. "He's a slam-dunk Hall of Famer," said Morris prophetically. "Forget what he needed to do, this is what he wanted to do. It was in his heart to do this."

Nevertheless, even before the redeeming hit, Winfield relished the move to Toronto and pondered its significance. "If my career had ended [before the move], I wouldn't have been really happy with what baseball dealt me. I would have had no fulfillment, no sense of equity, no fairness. I feel a whole lot better now about the way things have turned out."

* * * *

Dave Winfield played for several teams during his illustrious major league career. In 1983, as a member of the visiting New York Yankees, he succeeded in ruffling the feathers of a whole flock of Blue Jays fans at Toronto's Exhibition Stadium. While warming up between innings of the August 4 contest, a throw by Winfield struck and killed a seagull. Fans were not impressed, throwing debris and insults at the outfielder. New York manager Billy Martin was philosophical. "It's the only time he's hit the cutoff man all season," he deadpanned.

Later that day, the Ontario Provincial Police charged him with animal cruelty and only a $500 bond prevented him from becoming a jail bird. Yankee teammate Graig Nettles asked him if he had plead "gull-ty." Although charges were eventually dropped, and Winfield donated generously to a Toronto charity, the incident made Winfield Public Enemy Number One in Toronto. During every subsequent visit to the city, fans stood and flapped their arms derisively. Then, in 1992, he signed with the Jays as a designated hitter. Suddenly, he was a hero, and all was forgiven. When his game-winning two-run double in the 11th inning of Game Six of the World Series brought the Queen City its first World Championship, he became known as Mr. Jay.

Just goes to show that birds of a feather, eventually, flock together.

* * * *

The well-traveled Winfield once compared spring training past and present. "These days baseball is different," he said. "You come to spring training to get your legs ready, your arms loose, your agents ready, and your lawyer lined up."

* * * *

In 1991, while Winfield was still a member of the California Angels, he was hitting third in the lineup, in front of fellow slugger Dave Parker. It was a scary prospect for American League hurlers. Or, as Winfield put it, "You're going to hear pitchers saying, 'Nobody told me there'd be Daves like this.'"

* * * *

In Game One of the 1992 ALCS against the Oakland A's, fans showed up at SkyDome in gorilla suits and threw bananas to the fans in the left-field stands. Why?, you might well ask. They were responding to a challenge from Dave Winfield, who had called fans out for what he saw as a lack of enthusiasm. The fans held a sign that read DAVE WINFIELD SAYS GO BANANAS. The crowd did indeed go ape in cheering for the hometown nine. Even actors Michael J. Fox and John Candy joined in. Alas, it was all for naught as the Jays lost 4-3 in the Series opener.

ALVIS WOODS

April 7, 1977, was a day of "firsts,"and merely by coming to the plate as a pinch hitter for Steve Bowling, left fielder Woods made it into the Blue Jays history book. But what he did next underlined and highlighted that name, and that game. It was Opening Day, not only for the season, but for all the seasons to come in the city of Toronto. As if to add to the drama of the day, Woods homered in his first at-bat off Francisco Barrios of the visiting White Sox. He remained a member of the Blue Jays until 1982.

GREGG ZAUN

He has been called "the Don Cherry of baseball," not only for his strong opinions and his willingness to share them, but for his striking sartorial choices. His suits may not be quite as flamboyant as those sported by Grapes, but they stand out in a crowd. Montreal writer Ted Bird once mused, "One of these days, Gregg Zaun is going to be swallowed whole by his suit, and Jamie Campbell isn't even going to notice."

Gregg Zaun was the Baltimore Orioles' 17th round draft pick in the 1989 amateur draft and he first cracked the Orioles major league lineup in 1995. In 1997 he was a member of the World Series-champion Florida Marlins. He went on to play for 10 different teams in his 16-year career, his Toronto stint being from 2004-2008.

He was the everyday catcher for the Jays for most of that time period. He possessed a strong arm to second base and owns the Jays record for most runners caught stealing with 88.

* * * *

After crouching behind home plate for 18 innings in an early August game between the Blue Jays and California Angels in 2005, Jays catcher Gregg Zaun was understandably exhausted. "I definitely know one thing about Ernie Banks and his 'Let's play two' thing," he said. "Ernie Banks ain't never strapped on catcher's gear."

* * * *

If Matt Stairs had a kindred spirit in baseball, it would likely be Gregg Zaun. They were both down-and-dirty, no-nonsense players. As Stairs recalls:

"Gregg Zaun—the man we call Zauny Bench. We're good buddies. I think he just loves the game so much. I've known Gregg Zaun since back in the Baltimore Orioles days when he was with the Orioles and I was with the A's.

"Gregg Zaun was a hard-nosed worker. He was a student of the game because he made it so much easier on the pitching staff. He did so much homework on how to pitch to certain hitters and the pitchers just stuck on his back and he carried the day.

"I think he used his talents to the max. He was a guy that wasn't the big, tall, athletic-looking catcher, like Carlton Fisk. He wasn't one of the flashy receivers, but he had lots of other things going for him. He had the smarts and the talents to out-think hitters, and he worked very well with pitchers. It's kind of tough when you're 5'9". You know you have to work extra hard and battle. He did that and it worked out well."

* * * *

While with the Jays, Zaun had a small but dedicated group of followers who called themselves Zaunbie Nation. "They started wearing all these crazy ghoul masks," he told Collum Hughson at *mopupduty.com.* "I think there were like eight or nine of them. I wouldn't say it's grown. Every once and a while you'll see a sign, but it was pretty much eight guys that didn't even live in

Toronto. I figured while it was funny and somewhat popular—all eight of them—you might as well run with it."

* * * *

Zaun's mother told Alyson Footer of *MLB.com* that her son "was just a fun-loving, great kid." He once was caught trying to steal burritos out of the food machine at school "because he got his arm caught in it."

* * * *

What was Gregg Zaun's favorite TV show? If you were thinking *This Week in Baseball*, or even *The Walking Dead*, you'd be wrong. Zaun liked to relax after a long day at the ballpark by watching *Desperate Housewives*. And yes, he chewed tobacco while watching, but as he explained, "I used to chew tobacco when I watched any TV show." He has since quit the habit.

* * * *

Like Joe Garagiola, Zaun went from backup catcher to the broadcast booth. Garagiola once described his status as a second-fiddle catcher thusly: "What you are is a well-paid blowout patch." Zaun, a lifetime .252 hitter, once admitted, "There are weeks when I couldn't hit water if I fell out of a boat."

* * * *

In an interview with Clayton Richer of *baseballhotcorner.com* (April 26, 2012), Zaun was asked about the best and worst advice he had ever received from a manager. "The best and worst advice I ever got from a manager came from the same man at the same time. 'Get on the plane and hide from the GM for 6 months, because if he knows I put you on this team, he'll fire me.'" It came from Jim Leyland of the Florida Marlins.

* * * *

When Zaun retired from playing ball and turned to broadcasting, his Zaunbie Nation fan club grew into the Toronto community charity known as Zauntourage. He is also involved with Right to Play and was instrumental in the Uganda Project, which raised funds to send a Canadian Little League team to that African nation to play "the game that never was" against the first African Little League team to qualify for the Little League World Series. Because of a lack of verifiable birth certificates in this third-world nation, the Ugandans had been blocked from playing. His charity, the Gregg Zaun Foundation, works with children in need.

"Going to Uganda was a thrill. We set out to do some good by righting a wrong," Zaun explained. "I think one of the most important commodities in the world [is] the dream of a child. They need to be preserved. I think we made some dreams come true."

* * * *

ACKNOWLEDGMENTS

I have been fortunate enough to watch the Toronto Blue Jays grow from a fledgling expansion franchise to a two-time World Champion and a perennial playoff contender. Canada is and always will be a hockey nation, but the Blue Jays have made amazing inroads, and when they won back-to-back World Championships in 1991 and '92, the coast-to-coast celebrations rivaled any that a Stanley Cup championship has inspired. The Jays have enriched the Canadian sports scene and made it a part of our shared experience as Canadians.

I would like to thank the following people for their help in the writing of this book:

Shawn Ells, Matt Stairs, Jason Hockley, David Hockley, Paul Henderson, Curt Schilling, Maxwell Kates, Jerry Howarth, Vernon Wells Sr., Vernon Wells Jr., Paul Hodgson, Scott Russell, and editor Julie Ganz.

BIBLIOGRAPHY

Bell, George and Elliott, Bob. (1998). *Hardball.* Key Porter Books Limited.

Broomer, Stuart. (1994). *Paul Molitor: Good Timing.* ECW Press

Kendall, Brian. (1995). *Great Moments in Canadian Baseball.* Lester Publishing.

Brunt, Stephen. (1993). *Second to None: The Roberto Alomar Story.* Viking.

Humber, William. (1995). *Diamonds of the North: A Concise History of Baseball in Canada.* Oxford University Press.

Will, George F. (1998). *Bunts.* Scribner.

Shearon, Jim. (1994). *Canada's Baseball Legends.* Malin Head Press.

Stieb, Dave with Boland, Kevin. (1986). *Tomorrow I'll Be Perfect.* Doubleday Canada Ltd.

Luciano, Ron and Fisher, David. (1990). *Baseball Lite.* Bantam Books.

Williams, Ted and Prime, Jim. (1995). *Ted Williams' Hit List*. Stoddart Publishing.

Fidlin, Ken and Thornhill, Fred. (1989). *The Official Blue Jays Album, A Dozen Years of Baseball Memories*. Seal Books.

Whitt, Ernie and Cable, Greg. (1989). *Catch: A Major League Life*. Random House of Canada Ltd.

OTHER SOURCES

Lion's Den U

Sourcebook, The Official Magazine of the Toronto Blue Jays (1988)

The Sporting News, 1988 yearbook

ESPN, The Magazine, July 9, 2001 (Bruce Feldman on Carlos Delgado)

Sports Illustrated magazine (Ron Fimrite on Dave Stieb)

The Toronto Sun

The Toronto Star

The Globe and Mail

The National Post

Sportsnet Magazine

The New Yorker (May 6, 2013) *Oddballs,* by Ben McGrath

SABR piece on Alan Ashby, by Max Kates

NOTE: Every effort was made to identify and credit reporters and/or authors whose player interviews were referenced in this book. If any source was inadvertently omitted in the bibliography and sources, please contact the author or publisher and they will be added in subsequent editions.

Writer Bio: Jim Prime is the author of almost 20 baseball and hockey books. He lives in New Minas, in the heart of the beautiful Annapolis Valley of Nova Scotia.